CH00690645

" And now I have to confess the
unpardonable and the scandalous.
I am a happy man. And I am going
to tell you the secret of my happiness.
It is quite simple. I love mankind.
I love love. I hate hate.
I try to understand and accept. „

– JEAN COCTEAU

This book is dedicated to the memory of **Joe Crow**

" A small group of thoughtful
people could change the world.
Indeed, it's the only thing
that ever has. „

– MARGARET MEAD

acknowledgements

We are so thankful to all who have helped us be the people we are today. To our families; we are grateful for the love, support and lessons taught that allowed us the freedom to create the amazing lives we are now living. We honor you all.

To the supporters of Quest Teen Leadership; there are too many names to mention individually. To those who gave their time and hearts to the development of the program, countless hours of volunteering and financial support, we humbly bow to you and your service. To the thousands of teens that participated in the program who so openly shared their stories, volunteered countless hours and continue to live the lessons taught in the program, we honor you. Everything we did and everything that all Quest supporters gave was for you. You are our future and knowing that, we feel much hope in what is possible.

Think or Swim, LLC
5760 Legacy Dr. Ste. B3-326
Plano, TX 75024
www.thinkorswim.tv
info@thinkorswim.tv

Design by Erica A de Flamand / Summer House Creative, Inc.
www.the-summerhouse.com

Editing by Beth Howard
www.bethhowardwriter.com

Printed in the United States of America

table of contents

What every extraordinary person **KNOWS**

think or**swim**

LESLIE PALMER

SEAN EUBANKS

" If the only tool you have is a hammer, you tend to see every problem as a nail. „

— ABRAHAM MASLOW

Why We Wrote This Book

Leslie

I love instant gratification. Who doesn't? There are books that tell you how to lose weight in 17 days, remove wrinkles in 30 days, and find a man in 10 days. There are books about making a million in 24 months, clearing the clutter in your house in 24 hours, or how to travel the world in 24 days. Most of these books I own and some made a huge difference in my life. But when it came to the really important things, like surviving the death of a spouse, handling my son's mental illness, losing a job and my dreams, I didn't find a quick fix on the bookshelves.

Instead I rolled up my sleeves and did the work. I spent years reading and studying and attending workshops. Every new discovery sent me to my knees in anguish. WHY DIDN'T SOMEONE TEACH THIS TO ME IN MY YOUTH? Learning about self-awareness, emotional intelligence and the power of thought turned my life upside down. So much so that I sold everything I owned and created a methodology for teaching it to teens. The method was so simple, that not only did they quickly understand the concepts, but they were able to immediately implement them in their daily lives. This program was called Quest Teen Leadership and thousands of teens around the country have graduated from the two-day workshop, which is now being offered by the Think or Swim Team.

The adults that were using the program were also having results in their lives that were game changers. On June 13, 2011, I got a Facebook message from an amazing man that had staffed a teen workshop years ago in Dallas, TX. He had created an extremely successful business in the previous 4 years and gave this program much of the credit. "I'd like to sponsor a teen workshop and get involved again with this amazing work," read the comment.

After hours of conversation we decided to write a book and expand on the work of the trainings. We wrote the majority of this book in eight weeks, and began designing cell phone Apps so that readers can easily use these tools on the go. It is our intention to make implementing these concepts into your daily life as simple as possible.

Each principle in the book is first explained and then followed up with an example from my life and one from Sean's. From our two, very different paths, you will be able to see how we use these lessons daily.

We really spilled our guts in this book in order to show you the difference these tools and principles can make in the average person's life. We believe that life IS an amazing adventure. Will you create it or will it create you?

Sean

I knew that the key to what Leslie was teaching in her work-shops was the experiential learning piece. Learning by doing instead of by listening to tapes or reading a book makes all the difference in the world. I'd read about or was aware of some of the basic concepts in this book, but being a part of the trainings and seeing the transformation of the teens is what really hit home. The more I taught, the more I learned. After the 3rd training, I had seen enough of the results to make a commitment in my own life to follow this path. Little did I know, within a year, I would be put to the test in both the business world and my relationship with my family.

At the time I was a partner in a start-up company with no capital, no experience, and lots of debt from mistakes made in our first year in business. After applying the principles in this book, I watched my business become very profitable and continue to grow year after year. At the same time, I was able to deal with unimaginable suffering and tragedy within my family. I use these tools to grow stronger and smarter every day and want to be clear that I am a work in progress. Understanding how to use the tools – Be the Observer, Neutral Event, Forgiveness, and Intention – keeps things in perspective for me and allows me to thrive in circumstances that otherwise might make me quit.

Anyone who has had the privilege to meet and spend time with Leslie Palmer would know as I do that she is a beautiful person, a gifted teacher, and an incredibly strong woman.

I enjoyed presenting in the trainings with her and knew that what she was teaching was so simple, yet so profound. I knew then, as now, that every teen and every person, for that matter, could learn from the trainings and improve their lives. When I contacted her earlier this year, my intention was to sponsor a teen training for 50 kids in the Plano area. It would be a chance to reconnect with Leslie, and I'd also gladly volunteer my time to be an assistant trainer with her. Our talks quickly escalated into teaching and sharing this message with a broader audience, a focus on all people, not just teenagers. It would take some adjustments and have a different feel, but we could do it.

What I know about people is that everyone has a story and that all of us have trials and tribulations. If we understood and practiced how to shape our thoughts to create the life we wanted, we would all be a lot better off. I made the commitment to write this book and share some of my story with you so that you would be inspired to take action using the tools provided. You will see that with every tool, you will be given the opportunity to connect with someone in your life.

My vision for everyone who reads this book is twofold: First that you embrace being the observer of your own life, get clarity on what you want your legacy to be, and that you take action to create the life you want to have. Second is that each person who reads this: connects with, acknowledges, and forgives five people in their lives. In doing this, you will discover that you are a gift to this world, your friends, and your family. I hope you do the work and can only smile in excitement as you discover what's next for you in this life.

"It is by going down into the abyss that we recover the treasures of life. Where you stumble there lies your treasure. „

– JOSEPH CAMPBELL

Our Journeys To Here

Leslie

How can a person reach the age of forty and still have no idea how life works? Let me rephrase this, how did I reach the age of forty and not only NOT know how I got here, but have no clue as to how I was going to navigate the next forty years. Sure, I was rolling with the punches. But I felt as if life was happening to me and I had no say. Where was the instruction book? All I wanted was to be a good person, to be happy, to have love, to have an exciting career and friends, while having fun and creating world peace. Is that so much to ask? If God can create this magnificent universe, create minds that run like mainframe computers, couldn't He at least have given us a manual on how to survive depression, heartbreak, job loss, and an empty 401K? This is not a rhetorical question. How often do you hear people say, "I wish we had come with an owner's manual?" Or parents say to their children, "It's not like you came with instructions. I did the best I could with what I knew." It is enough for most people to realize, at the end of the day, that they did their best. It was also enough for me until I reached the age of forty. I guess you could say I had a mid-life crisis. All I know is that I became extremely restless. There was a burning in my belly that there must be more and, since I have a bit of the type A in me, I decided to actively pursue the answers.

In all honesty, this was more than your average mid-life crisis. Although I was on a mission to figure out what was next for my life, I was in the midst of two really big emotional struggles. My husband and I were getting a divorce, and my 19-year-old son David was in a recovery program for alcoholism. Out of that program came many disclosures. My heart was broken by the pain my son had endured, and I felt that I must take some action to heal my heart as he was so bravely doing the work to heal his own.

I am a reader and that was where I started my journey. I read hundreds of books (books written by people much smarter than myself): books about psychology, the workings of the mind, emotional intelligence, personal development, leadership, self-awareness, and ancient philosophies. I tried therapy and it was great. I looked at and began to heal my father/mother psychological wounds. I hired a coach. I took many personality tests and other "What-should-I-be-when-I-grow-up?" profiling mechanisms. I joined an intensive, year-long Bible study that had a very intellectual approach to the scriptures. I attended workshops and read, read, read. Then somewhere along the way I woke up. I really woke up.

Through all of this studying, I spent some time trying

to figure out exactly who I wanted to be. You can't get where you are going if you don't know your destination. In Abraham Maslow's discussions on his pyramid of self-actualization, I was given an example of the type of person I wanted to become. "She would be comfortable in her skin, someone who wouldn't worry about what other people thought. She would be caring and loving and empathetic and would never judge others as she has a knowing that basically we are all the same. People would naturally be drawn to her. She would be so clear in her purpose that she would be self-motivating. She would manage her emotions in a way that would serve her life, not that she wouldn't get angry or sad, but it would always be appropriate to the situation and would not control her. She would love herself so much that loving others would be natural. She would have a sense of humor and be able to laugh at herself, knowing that all was perfect and as it should be. She would know that anything was possible and would see life as an adventure and as a choice."

Part of my "waking up" included knowing that I wanted to teach these lessons to others. My initial intent was to create something so simple that I could teach it to teenagers. They are my first love. The teen years are so critical, and most adults I know can hardly stand to be in the presence of teenagers. Really, people, is it so hard to remember the hell that high school was for so many of us? If you weren't the one being made fun of, you were probably one of the ones who caused the pain. Or at a minimum, you were on the fringe of one of those groups. Although I was not picked on, I remember with shame ignoring others who were taunting my friends. Most of us were completely lost. Lost to who we were, where we were going, and how to be happy. Like that was a choice! Our happiness rested daily on who sat with us in the cafeteria, whether or not it was a good-hair day, or if our jeans made our butt look big. What would it have been like if we had been comfortable in our own skin and not worried what others thought? What if we had use of tangible tools that would help us make friends and get along with our parents? You know, the instructions that should have been in the manual we got at birth?

With the help of many, over 4,000 teens around the country have attended the self-awareness trainings that I spoke of earlier. Over the seven years that these workshops have been offered, I have faced the challenge of explaining to schools and parents the value of these principles. Although you will have an opportunity to learn these lessons from this book, there is nothing that can take the place of experiencing these life lessons first hand. Experiential learning is so critical for true understanding, and it is the method we use to teach teens in our two-day workshops. Experiential learning is learning by enacting the behavior in question. When we learn by doing, we retain it, much like learning to ride a bike. No one gives you a book at the age of six and asks you to read it, take a test and then apply it to riding a bike. You learn by getting on and falling off and getting on and falling off. And then there's the joy of riding those first shaky few yards!

For those of you who have not been on a bike in years, just imagine putting your hands on the handle bars and you will know exactly what to do next. YOU DO NOT HAVE TO THINK ABOUT IT. It is automatic. When you learn by DOING you retain far more information than if you read, listen to someone lecture about a subject or watch someone performing the activity. There's an old saying, "Teach me and I'll forget. Show me and I may remember. Involve me and I'll understand." This book along with the Think or Swim Apps will give you the opportunity to be involved in the process.

Although I am still striving to be the "she" I mentioned above, if I had not created the seven steps mentioned in this book's lessons, I am not sure I would have survived the challenges of the past ten years. Many of the people that have experienced our workshops and coaching are truly embracing an intentional life. Once you understand the principles, it is simple. If God in his infinite wisdom did not give us a manual, He did give us an internal knowledge of how to grow and evolve. That is the secret. We have an INTERNAL compass. The answer is within.

This handbook teaches people how to look within and find those answers. Being the nerd (in the best sense of the word) that I am, a part of me thinks that a thousand pages covering the internal locus of control, Maslow's self-actualization pyramid, and the role of the amygdala would serve this topic better. We are writing this book so that you don't have to swim through pages of other people's theories. I am sharing a life manual that works for me, i.e. a summation of all the brilliant writings that I have devoured. I am not a therapist or a great philosopher, nor do I hold a Ph.D. I am an average, middle-aged woman who wants to support others on their path. Maybe this book and these tools will give you some insight. Hopefully you can benefit from my years of study and exploration. Although this is not The Answer, it can possibly be an answer to further assist you on your own journey.

....

Sean

Everything I was reading and listening to at the time was telling me to relax. All these books were saying in their own way to stop and smell the roses. I was 30 years old, had a college degree, had traveled around the world, was making six figures, and was finally debt-free. This was a long way from the trailer park where I was raised as a young child. My family was proud of me. I had just started my own nonprofit organization and was up to big things helping martial artists get funding for college. Nonetheless, I was resigned to the fact that being an adult was going to be incredibly boring at times and everybody had to put a certain amount of time in a cubicle to prove their worth. I'd move up the corporate ladder, invest in real estate, travel when I wanted, and life would be good. I was my own worst critic and always expected myself to do well. I was an attractive, college educated, white man in America. There was no excuse for me not to live the dream. My online dating profile at the time said I was "intellectually curious, goofy, and smart." What's not to love about that? I was taking a medication called lithium to stabilize my mood and I couldn't trust myself without it, but that really wasn't important at the time. I read every book I could get my hands on. I was in every sales seminar I could get my company to pay for, and I even used my vacation time to sneak off and get a commercial real estate designation. I knew I wanted more, but I didn't even know what I wanted more of.

My competitive drive and tireless work ethic allowed me to remain a top earner and constantly work on side projects, too. I was bored, but I thought to myself, I really should slow down and just be grateful. I should get married, start a family and move into a track home. It would give me something to focus on other than myself, and my grandma would stop asking me if I'm gay every Thanksgiving. But then again, my grandfather might stop giving me that secret thumbs up and that Cheshire-cat smile I came to know and love. I knew that most people wished they had it as good as I did.

In order to live a balanced life, I needed to work on being less selfish and to improve my relationship with God. I'd go to a different church every weekend trying to find one I liked. My parents were born-again Christians, and all of my friends seem to find peace in the church, so I'd go, too.

The point I'm trying to make is the concepts in this book did not give me a competitive drive or a will to succeed.

These traits were part of my core. But the concepts presented in this book and practiced in the trainings are what made me the success I am today. I got my first look at these concepts at a Quest Teen Leadership workshop mentioned above. I had the opportunity to staff a workshop where the kids attending ranged from the very poor to kids who were from affluent private schools in Plano, Texas. What I learned confirmed what I already knew: The teenage years are a challenge no matter what side of the tracks you live on. I saw teens' lives transformed and I saw them truly waking up. Lives were changed. The concepts were simple enough for them and for me to understand. I learned that I could not only observe my thoughts, but I could CHOOSE them too. I became aware of how I judge others and how to forgive them. The awareness and information in itself was priceless, but the "what to do next" is where the real benefit kicked in.

I had the opportunity to apply these concepts at a time when all I had was my thoughts. In 2008, the real estate market crashed and I lost my job. A side business venture also lost a lot of money. I was in serious debt with no income, and my family was torn apart by an unthinkable event. I literally had nothing but my thoughts. That's the truth. If I had not been given the tools written about in this book, I really don't know if I would have been able to make it. Now I know that no matter what might come along, I will be ready for it. I'm ready no matter what happens next. I will always get to choose.

HOW TO USE THIS BOOK

It is our intention that this book gives you information, examples, and tools that will support you in creating the life you desire. It is our intention that the information is conveyed and laid out in such a simple format that you can, after reading, use as a reference. The format will be as follows.

THE LESSON	Will explain how we, Leslie and Sean, believe you can best utilize the Think part of our lives. These lessons, numbers 1 – 7, build upon each other.
A STORY FROM LESLIE	The story will reflect how she did or did not use the principles in the preceding lesson.
LESLIE OBSERVING	This is where we have the opportunity to view our stories with 20/20 hindsight. Being the observer is the ability to be self-aware and will be taught in detail in Lesson #2.
A STORY FROM SEAN	Sean will use the same concept as Leslie, but with his own style and unique circumstances.
SEAN OBSERVING	This is where Sean will use self-awareness to assess his story.
THE APP	This is where you will have the opportunity to experience an application that will teach you the lesson in an experiential way. Apps are used for everything these days and the written version in the book will assist in integrating the lesson into your life quickly.

" The space for what we
want is being occupied
by the things we have
settled for. ,,

– ANONYMOUS

Your Thoughts Create Your Life

You've probably heard statements like the one above many times in your life, especially in the last few years. You have also heard about the power of positive thinking. I'm sure, to some degree, we all get that concept. If you think positively about life you will basically be a happier person and people will like you more. It feels very Pollyanna-ish. Let's face it, some of us do not naturally have a sunny disposition, and some of us see life with the glass half empty. But are you open to the possibility that your thoughts are creating your life, ABSOLUTELY and COMPLETELY? That not only your perceptions and your attitude, but your thoughts are literally creating the events in your day?

Let's look at Albert Einstein's famous quote: "The biggest decision you will ever make in your life is whether you live in a hostile world or a friendly world." There is an old story about two people that move into a new town. They are both walking around the town square when one approaches a local who is also taking a walk. He introduces himself and says to the local, "I just moved to your town and was wondering what the people are like here." The local turns to him and asks, "What were the people like in the town you left?" "Well," says the newcomer, "they were just awful. They were so nasty and rude. I didn't have any friends because everyone was so selfish and hateful." "Well," says the local, "that is exactly how you will find the people here."

As the local continues walking down the street the other newcomer to the town approaches him. "Excuse me sir," says the second newcomer, "I just moved to your town and was wondering what the people are like here." The local asks her the same question he asked the first newcomer. "What were the people like in the town where you used to live?" "Oh my," says the second newcomer, "they were amazing. Everyone was so sweet. My neighbors were always helping out and bringing me freshly baked goods and even the strangers you passed on the street were friendly and kind." "Well," says the local, "that is exactly how you will find the people here."

Whenever we tell this story in a workshop, people always get upset and say, "Why did the local lie to the two visitors?" "He told one guy the town was horrible and the other that the town was great." Really, is that what you heard? Review the statement. He told each of them that they would FIND the new town exactly like the town where they used to live. You see. THEY are the ones that decide what the new town will be like. They decide if they live in a hostile world or a friendly world. You decide how your world will be. No one can MAKE you think anything. They can influence you. Your past and your life circumstances can influence you. But NO ONE controls your thoughts. At any moment you can think whatever you want to think. People that are loving and open will attract loving and open people into their lives, and vice versa. Once you get that, I mean really get it at your core (as deep inside of you as possible), then you can decide the life you are going to have and the world in which you are going to live.

So let's get back to this *Your-Thoughts-Create-Your-Life* business. A few examples of life's tragedies are:

- I lost my job through corporate cutbacks
- My child died of leukemia
- I broke my leg and wasn't able to go on a vacation
- My husband left me

Of course you will say that you did not cause any of these things to happen. There are always events in life that happen where you literally have no conscious or physical control over them. But you do, at all times have control over your thoughts. We are suggesting that the physical things, places, and events that surround our life are only as horrible or wonderful as we make them. We do not expect you to understand this now, but we ask you to trust that Lesson #1 is the foundation of all the lessons in this book and the foundation of our experience on this earth as humans. We are asking you to trust. We are asking you to commit to reading the entire book. We are asking you to take a risk. **What do you have to lose?**

Leslie — **YOUR THOUGHTS CREATE YOUR LIFE**

As a sixteen-year-old, I could best be described as a lump of tofu. At sixteen, I did not know what tofu was, but I, like tofu, was definitely something that simply absorbed the flavor of whatever food was placed around it in the bowl of life. I had no thoughts of my own. I did not know that there was a ME. I simply did what I was told, followed the path of least resistance, and blended in.

I guess I was smart. At least, I was always placed in the advanced classes in school. But I never really thought about it. I simply did what everyone else did, which was study, show up for class, and answer questions only when I was asked.

I went to Garinger High School, a fairly middle-class school at the time, in Charlotte, N.C. In tenth grade I was in Mrs. Travis' Gifted or SAT English class, as it was called back in the day. I always did my homework, and I made mostly A's, and never got in trouble. My teachers liked me. Up until that time it was easy to make A's. For every class there was a book. The teacher would teach a subject. You would read the pages in the textbook and be given a test on it. This I could do. It required nothing from me and, remember, I did not know there was a ME. I could do this all day long.

But writing was different. I had to pull something original out of myself (the ME that didn't exist). To add to the pressure, there was the concept of PLAGIARISM. I had to write a paper about a subject, but I could not copy what other people had written about the subject. Gee, how the heck do you do that? This was terrifying to me, because I would not lie, cheat or do anything that would send me to hell. You might laugh about some sweet, young teenager worrying about something she did in class causing her to go to hell, but I worried about hell every day. Remember, I'm tofu and the majority of my time out of school was spent in church. There are many things I loved about my church and my faith as a child, but the fear of God was the underlying motivator in all decisions. That one concept did more to flavor my existence than anything else. I felt I must always be vigilant and not do anything in any moment that would cause me to go to hell when I died. That's quite a lot for a 16-year-old to worry about.

At the end of 10th grade, Mrs. Travis, my English teacher, had given me an A on my report card, but when she handed back the term papers written in that last month of school, she did not return mine. Back in the '70s, tenth grade was the first year you had to write a term paper and for those of us going to college, we knew that writing a paper well was very important. At the end of class, I went up to my teacher and asked why she hadn't returned my paper. She just laughed and said, "Honey, you don't need to see it. Let's just face it, you can't write." She just continued laughing and waived me off.

Now, although I was a good student, the term paper was a third of our grade. If she thought it was awful and gave me a grade of a D or F, she could not have given me an A on my report card. In her mind, she was doing me a favor by acting like the term paper did not exist, so I could keep a good GPA. What she did not realize is that her words changed the course of my life. I was DEVASTATED, I mean really devastated. I took her words to be absolute truth. From that moment on I decided that I could not write. I was terrified every time I had to write anything; an essay, a thank-you letter, or even a note to a friend. Her words literally paralyzed me and this lasted for over 20 years. I may not be Hemingway, but I can write. Maybe it is because I really pay attention to how certain things are written—business letters, thank you notes, etc. – but I probably would have progressed to my current skill level in two to three years had I not accepted the curse of her words. I gave this woman one of the keys to my life. I gave her the power to affect my college career, my business career, and even my personal correspondence.

The seed that she planted in 1976 sprouted into a huge roadblock in the course of my life. Because I accepted that I could not write as fact, I got a D-minus in freshman English at UNC-Chapel Hill, which was one of the factors in my dropping out of college. I had wanted to be a psychiatrist since I was a young child, and my love came mostly from years of watching "The Bob Newhart Show." I WAS Lucy with the 5-cent sign of Charles Schultz's classic comic strip, "Peanuts," doling out advice to all my friends. I would have made an amazing therapist and because that desire was so core in my heart, I have basically ended up in that role through my workshops and coaching. But, I allowed those words "You are a terrible writer" to derail me from my dream and send me on another completely different life path.

Your thoughts create your life, even when you are given those thoughts from someone else.

LESLIE OBSERVING

Being the Observer is a huge concept in the workshops and in this book. Everything that happens in life is simply an opportunity to notice, to stop and view with no judgment. Witnessing is the concept of self-awareness, the ability to view your thoughts and actions as separate from you. When we stop and notice, we become masters of what we create. In my story above, I now realize that I did not have to accept the "curse" from my teacher. It was not fact; it was her perception, based on my very first paper. At another level, I can also notice that I had a pattern of passively accepting the opinions and beliefs of those around me. This is just me Being the Observer. But with this awareness, I can monitor my choices and decide whether I am doing what I believe or what I think others want me to believe.

Sean — YOUR THOUGHTS CREATE YOUR LIFE

I had trained for this moment all of my life. I had chased this ghost all year long. The point standings in every martial-arts magazine publication would show my name or his as the #1 fighter in North America. We had never met face-to-face in the ring. We had seen each other's names in the magazines, but had never had the chance to fight, that is, before today. We had been competing across the country at different tournaments accumulating points with one goal: Win the #1 slot. My dad had flown with me to the tournament in Washington, DC and he would watch me have my moment in person. I was in perfect shape. At the age of 18, I had dedicated 7 years to training, fighting, and dominating the competition at the state level. I was getting ready to beat the nation's best and expose the paper tiger that held my national ranking. My feet were fast; my hands were ready to deliver a Texas-sized beat-down. I took pride in my state's reputation for producing fighters. Everybody knew that we liked to fight.

This was my day. I rushed through the Kata events with my focus on the fact that he was here and I was going to not only beat him, but send a message. In my mind, I visualized that we'd be a featured fight on stage, and thousands of people would gather to see this Texas fighter take down the number #1 ranked fighter in North America. I was eager, happy, and a little arrogant. No one could handle my speed. This was what I did and I was trained by one of the best instructors in the country and sparred every day with one of its' best black belts. I'd done this hundreds of times and KNEW from past confirmations that I was not only the best in Texas, but more talented than most of my competition and hungrier to win than any of them. My thoughts focused on hitting him as hard as I could and hurting him with my power, and then he'd be afraid to open up and I'd walk right through him. My mind wandered: Would this be a fight that would make the tournament highlights? Could this be shown on TV? Could I drop him with a jump turn sidekick and then high-five my buddy, Bruce, or lay him out flat on his back when I brought an axe-kick down on top of his head gear and slammed through his chest with my heel? Would Bruce, my best friend and training partner, be able to see me light him up? Maybe not. But my dad would film it and we'd laugh about it on the plane ride home. That was for sure. My thoughts were on HOW I'd beat him, not IF I'd beat him.

I breezed through my first three fights, and it was all I could do to not look past them to my prize. He won his first two fights with ease. He almost lost his third. I was on the edge of my seat. Was this knucklehead going to ruin my chance to prove I'm the best by losing to a lesser opponent? I cheered for him to win and KNEW it was my time. The arena was loud. My dad had seen me fight a thousand times at hundreds of tournaments over the years, but this day was special. He'd get to see me prove I was the best in the country. I was 2 minutes away from accomplishing my goal and this was to be a celebration of the last 7 years of training. After today, I could claim to have beaten the best in the country. I relished the underdog role and knew after today, they would give this Texas fighter his due. My instructor would be proud. Bruce would celebrate with me. I'd be the best in the country in two short minutes.

Eighteen feet away from me, he stood with his red and blue gi—the martial arts uniform. His entourage, loud and almost forcefully superficial, made it clear that a fighter from Team Metro was stepping into the ring to compete. He paced back and forth taking long strides with quick turns and glaring at me with every step. On the other side of the ring, I bounced side-to-side, arms at my side, facing him with my chest out. A big smile across my face, mouthpiece almost falling out, shaking my head yes...yes, it's about to go down.

But inside my head something very different was going on. I knew, "I can't beat this guy." The minute I saw him walk to the ring with his over-the-top entourage, I knew, "I'm going to lose." We met in the middle to touch gloves. I had one last thought race through my head right before the referee said go, "I can't win," I thought. "I can't beat him." And so I didn't.

I had trained seven years for this moment. I had beaten hundreds of opponents in the previous years. I was ready in every way. I was shocked and looking for an answer. What just happened? Did I lose my mind? I just quit. I gave that away, and I didn't know why or how. My dad told me I came out flat and he thought I should have won. That was all he said, but he looked at me with a long pause, almost as if he were trying to determine if I was sick. He knew I wasn't myself, but for some reason I thought he might have known I decided I couldn't win. To me, the thoughts in my head were so loud I actually worried that my dad might have heard them!

I never had the chance to fight that opponent again as we both fought in different regions of the country. I won 90% of my fights for the remainder of the year and never again made the mistake of stepping into the ring with the thought, "I am going to lose." I still have that plaque that says #2-ranked fighter in North America, and although it celebrates my national ranking, it means something much more to me. It reminds me that my thoughts control my life. Henry Ford said, "Whether you think you can or you think you can't, you're right."

SEAN OBSERVING

Let me be clear that THINKING you are going to win a match doesn't always make it so. But there is a very clear difference in my going into that match confident and still being beaten because my opponent was just better than me and my giving up. Because that is what happened: I gave up. I became intimidated by his entourage and his confidence. Having the OBSERVER tool and understanding why I default to thinking I'm not good enough would have changed the course of that day, and the story I tell myself about my life. I had the talent to beat him, but instead, I let my thinking beat me.

APPLICATION
Your Thoughts Create Your Life – Law

This concept is the foundation for EVERYTHING in this book. Lesson 1 is not really a tool. It is a knowing or belief system that you must accept like the law of gravity. It IS a law. It flows (like water) under all the other laws and tools provided.

In this chapter, you have read examples, stories, and quotes that confirm Your Thoughts Create Your Life. You may not accept this premise now, but if you practice the exercises and lessons in this book, you will absolutely begin to see its' truth. The exercise below will give you an experiential way of understanding this law. As we explained earlier, it is learning by doing. We hope that you will take the time to complete the exercises as they can all be done fairly quickly and many of them need only to be done once. When you understand the mechanism, you should be able to practice the concept when you need it in a few seconds.

EXERCISE: Your Thoughts Create Your Life

SUPPLIES: Body of water (pool, ocean, hot tub, bath)

Creed (highlighted below)

APPROX. TIME: 4 minutes

PURPOSE: To create a knowing in your innermost being that you are not your thoughts, that you are the observer, the witness to your thoughts, and that your thoughts are literally the engine or fire that creates and runs your life.

ACTION: Choose a body of water where you will be able to immerse yourself completely for as long as you can comfortably hold your breath (30 seconds). Make sure you will be uninterrupted for at least 5 minutes. Read the Creed below and have an understanding of it before immersing yourself in the water. Do the process thoughtfully and intentionally and allow this knowing or law to become a part of your life and your new way of thinking.

TONE: Hyper-aware of the physical sensations of being under water – muffled hearing, blurry vision, pressure in your ears, no sense of smell, feeling of separation from the world

YOUR THOUGHTS CREATE YOUR LIFE CREED

Since I am able to step back and view my thoughts from a distance,
I know that the I that is me is not my thoughts
My thoughts are the engine that run my life.
The observer or witness that is me can control my thoughts
and lead them in whatever direction I choose.
I am the director of my thoughts and therefore my life.

....

DEBRIEF: Can you feel the separation between you and your thoughts? Do you recognize the engine that is your thoughts is rarely silent and will run your life without your input? Knowing the "I" that is you can, with some practice, be aware and control your thoughts will put you in the drivers' seat of your life. This knowing is the flow of water running beneath you at all times.

TAKEAWAY: I accept as Law that my thoughts create my life and use this law as the foundation for intentionally creating the life I desire.

" Be careful how
you interpret life,
it is that way. „

– ERICH HELLER

Be The Observer

Your Thoughts Create Your Life...all the time. To know what you are thinking, you learn to **Be the Observer** – to step back and view.

Many of the great leaders that we admire are self-aware, which simply means that they are conscious, most of the time, that they are creating their life in every moment. Observing your life is the crux of self-awareness, the only way to consciously create the life you truly desire. The most important component of this lesson is that you must be an observer with no judgment. Remember a witness in a trial simply states the facts, doesn't add his opinion or enhance the story, just states the facts. We will use the term NOTICE as a "stop-and-pay-attention" sign to have us be the observer.

Let's practice what Being the Observer might look like in your life. We are going to ask you to step back, right in this moment, and be the witness or observer of you and your thoughts. Imagine your day thus far as if you were watching a movie. Picture yourself getting out of bed, eating breakfast, brushing your teeth. Can you remember what you were thinking? "I need to get a haircut, I have so much to do today, geez, I have to lose 20 pounds."

Now as the observer, you are viewing these movements and thoughts with no judgment. Imagine your observer as a little "mini-me" like the mini Mike Meyers in the "Austin Powers" movies. Picture your "mini-me" sitting on your shoulder (a two-inch version of you) and, with no judgment, view your day and your thoughts. The ability to do this one thing, to separate yourself from your thoughts is huge. This is the first step to becoming self-actualized or becoming that amazing person who is comfortable in their skin, never worries what others think, and is clear in their purpose and their values.

Folks, we are NOT our thoughts or our bodies or our stuff. We are the observer, and from this place of no judgment, we can create the lives of our dreams. But we must first learn to NOTICE. How can we ever make a change without the ability to see what needs to be changed? Why do great athletes have coaches? The athlete has the talent, but is often not able to see how they throw the ball or swing the club. They trust the coach to see it for them and direct them in becoming world class athletes. I believe that we have the innate ability to be our own coach. When we learn how to view our thoughts and assess whether they are in alignment with our dreams, then we can make intentional choices and create the life we desire. It is a simple formula. When we possess the ability to be the witness in our own lives then we can assess what's working and not working and make a shift.

Observing without judgment is the key to this lesson. Our experience of using this tool would often have us question ourselves with anger and judgment. "You idiot, why did you stay in that marriage?" or "You really believed what SHE said about you?" or "You should have quit that job years ago!" When we stopped that voice in our heads and just looked, really looked, at our actions and listened objectively to the conversations we were having with ourselves, then we could clearly see. We could see what had stopped us from creating amazing lives. Because if Your Thoughts Create Your Life then what the heck were we doing? Once we accepted as truth that our thoughts were creating our experience then the next logical step was to practice viewing our thoughts.

The tactic we use with our coaching clients is the practice of NOTICE. We will have them set up a system of times during the day where they simply stop and NOTICE, or view their actions and thoughts, with NO JUDGMENT. Once you become a master at this practice, and you really can, it is to simply check in to see if your actions and thoughts are in alignment with who you say you want to be in the world. There will be more about that to come. This handbook contains a simple formula, that when used consistently, keeps you on track with the life you want to create. I promise.

Remember when I joked about God not giving us a manual when we were born? I believe it is so that we make this journey of self-discovery. We have the answers inside of us, but until we can step back and objectively observe ourselves, we will continue like robots, unconscious and blind, stumbling around in the dark. The ability to be the observer is the first colossal step towards that "waking up." Some people have no idea what this means, and many spend most of their lives unconscious. But if you have gotten this far in the book, I ask that you continue (you did promise) and be open.

Leslie — BE THE OBSERVER

What the heck have I done? I am pregnant and my fate is sealed. Is this what happens when you simply float along and let life happen to you? I am 20 years old, living in a tiny apartment in Germany. My husband and I share a bathroom with four other families. Well, it is actually a toilet that is a hole with no water and no sink to wash your hands. We only have heat in the living room. Our kitchen is so cold that we put our food in the refrigerator so it won't freeze. We have an electric blanket on our bed and that is where I spend most of my time. We have no TV or phone and only a radio that picks up the U.S. Army station. My days are spent rolling a cart a mile to the train station to ride a train to the army base to wash clothes, buy food, and get books at the library. Reading is what I do with my time. I read 5-10 books a week. It keeps me sane.

But I am not sane. I have lost my chance to have the life I was supposed to have, the life all of my friends are having in the states—going to college, to the beach, and to parties. One year ago, I was a student at one of the top universities in the country. My dad was paying for my education, I had a car and friends, and I was on my way to creating a normal, successful life, a typical life for a young woman in the '70s. Did I choose this? Was I really that afraid of failing or succeeding in college? Why didn't someone tell me I was making a mistake? Where were the mentors, the grown-ups that are supposed to guide you? Even I, a big lump of tofu, can't continue this whining and blame.

I believed that if I had sex before marriage I would go to hell, so I got married. I believed if I opened my mind in college and listened to other ideas and philosophies, I might lose my soul, so I quit college.

I nearly escaped this fate. Two months ago I was flying across the ocean to Germany after spending the summer at home in Charlotte. It was an awesome summer. My husband had been sent to a special training school in Europe for two months so I came home to visit. I got a super, cool job and reconnected with all my old friends. They looked so good and were so happy. They had finished their sophomore year at college and were getting serious about majors, jobs, and life. What the heck had I done? None of my friends had quit school and gotten married. My peers were all smart, beautiful, and full of promise. I didn't fit in to the world of uneducated drop-outs who got married as teenagers. I was off-track. Something was desperately wrong. But maybe there was hope.

I planned my speech on the flight back to Germany. "It's not that I don't love you, but we are so young, and we both want so much. Let's cut our losses and get a divorce." I would simply share that with my husband and he would understand. He picked me up at the airport and he knew something was off. We made love, but it was strange, and we were very disconnected, and then we just started talking. He was feeling exactly like I was feeling. He had been in school for the past two months studying medicine (he wanted to be a doctor) and he knew that the next few years would be spent in the army and then school, and marriage just didn't make sense. Thank God. Whew. It was going to be ok. We were both going to have the futures we really wanted.

We did not take immediate action about how we would split up and we didn't feel any rush. We were just so glad we had escaped the fate you see in really bad "Lifetime" movies. But, one morning I was feeling really sick, and then I felt the same way the next morning and the next. After a quick visit to the Army doctor it was confirmed. I was pregnant. Oh, by the way, we used no contraception. I had always had irregular periods, and my doctor said I might have a hard time getting pregnant so we never bothered. That's tofu for you—passive, absorbing whatever is thrown its' way.

Everything is a choice, even not making a choice. Guess I'm going to be a mother. My fate is set.

LESLIE OBSERVING

Using the technique of OBSERVING, had I been self-aware at 19, I would have recognized that not having a father who loved and supported me would lead me to look to a male to fill that void. I would have recognized that I avoided making conscious decisions and choices. Being awake would have given me the awareness that I was creating my life with my choices and that it was time for me to get clear about what kind of life I wanted to have.

You might be saying to yourself, "Well, hindsight is 20/20," but I have seen teens in our workshops get really clear about who they want to be in the world and start practicing BEING THE OBSERVER every day. Even though I use this technique almost unconsciously, it doesn't mean that I don't make mistakes or that I have a perfect life. It simply means that I am awake enough to know that I am CHOOSING it all. I am never a victim to life. I can stop and notice what is working and not working and shift on a dime.

I do not regret for one minute having my son at such a young age. When I went back to college I was older and more aware of what I wanted. The journey of my life with my son has been such a gift. He is the person I most admire in the world. He is my hero.

Sean — **BE THE OBSERVER**

How'd it get this bad? Did I really deserve to be shipped off to Provo, UT, to an all-boys treatment center? My parents were really mad at me this time. Was it the fact that I got so drunk on my lunch break that I threw up during Spanish class and got expelled from school? Or the tattoo on my chest of the Tasmanian devil flipping the bird that really got under their skin? I'm 16. This is what kids do, right? I'm no criminal. Half of the kids in this treatment center are on their way to jail when they turn 18. This isn't the place for me. Mom and Dad will see the error of their ways and come around. I'll give them a few days.

Nine months later, I was discharged from the treatment center with a diagnosis of bipolar disorder, a prescription for lithium, and enough bad memories to keep me acting right for the foreseeable future.

For the next seventeen years, I took lithium three times a day and fully embraced that I was unbalanced and would lose my mind if I ever stopped taking the drug. I considered the dizziness, the upset stomachs, and the tremors as my sacrifice for having a normal life, a small price to pay. I had a full-time psychiatrist to keep filling my prescription, and Mom and Dad seemed to think this would keep me safe. I played football in high school and went on to play in college. Was it the drug, or did I simply figure out what worked and what didn't work?

As I got older and entered the corporate world, I brought the same crazy drive and energy to this playing field. So here's another example from my '20s: "Hey man, I'm the number one producer and the best this company has ever seen. When I close a loan, everybody around me knows it. I stand up in my cubicle and show my dance moves. Everybody on my team has seen the Euby Shuffle. I'd sell six loans before lunch to 'win' that little green, free-lunch ticket. Chicken quesadillas and one large Coke. That's right. I get mine for free because I'm that good.

I hate this, and I don't like myself, but I've come a long way baby and this is the best I'll ever have. I'm 20 pounds overweight, I drink a lot, but, hey, I'm young and single. That's what we do. I've got to be a man and suck it up. Besides, I don't have the capital to start my own business. It takes money to make money. I talked to that one bank, but they won't lend to me, so that's that. I had my own business, a maid service back in Austin and after three months got my vehicle repossessed and had to move back into my parents' house just to catch my breath. Thank God no one knows about that. I gave it my all. I worked so hard for those 3 months. How could I have spent that much on advertising! That was my fault, but those backstabbing subcontractors, if they had just been loyal, I'd be rich by now. Maybe I grew too fast. It's impossible to track all those customers at once.

Maybe my heart wasn't in it, but the bottom line is not everybody can own a business. I'm not smart enough to do all the things it takes to run a business. I'm an idiot when it comes to accounting, and I'm not sure people really like me enough to give me their business. At least I can say I tried it. I need to work for someone a lot longer and just save up my money. Besides, it's impossible to start a business in Austin. The market is terrible. I better play it safe and not take another risk. I'll be embarrassed if it doesn't work again. I'm the first college graduate in my family. I'll be damned if I ask my family for help again. I'll live on the street before I move back into my parent's house. What a nightmare that was!

Man, but look at me now: I'm driving a Range Rover Sport. This is the Promised Land! When I pull in this parking lot, everyone will know I'm successful. This is Dallas. Selling is easy to me. I'll coast for now and just sell. I'll do some stuff on the side and make extra money that way. Just diving into a business without deep pockets will never work."

This conversation dominated my life and was my reality until I recognized that I made this up based on one limited experience. I came to a point where I was so tired of working dead-end jobs and chasing commissions that I decided to dive in and try another business. I discovered right away that the sleepless nights and the fear of not paying my bills as a business owner was not any more frightening than when I worked as someone's employee. What I could control was my focus on doing what it took to generate revenue and make the next sale. None of the pain, self-doubt, discouragement, and sense of hopelessness about being able to run my own business was real. When I simply stepped back and began to observe what was working and not working, I could give those areas the necessary adjustments without all the drama and emotional carryover from the memory of my past failure.

Today, I am happy to report that my present company is on track to do $2 million in revenue this year. I would never have gotten to this point if I had not learned to ask the question, "what is working and what is not working?"

SEAN OBSERVING

I started my second business after I had learned the lessons in this book and was applying them daily in my life. The ability to be the observer and notice what worked and what didn't was the critical difference. When I understood that my thoughts came forth in my actions and energetically in my interactions with others was a huge wake-up moment for me. I literally use this tool multiple times a day. It is priceless.

APPLICATION
Be The Observer – Tool

This tool is the key to self-awareness. This tool is not a law because you have a choice whether to use it or not. It will do more for your life than winning the lottery. When you stop and notice, when you rewind the film and view your thoughts and actions, you then have the ability to make healthy decisions toward directing your life. Most people go through their lives asleep, never stepping back to objectively view their thoughts and actions. This exercise will teach you how to implement this practice into your life until it becomes second nature.

EXERCISE: Be The Observer

SUPPLIES: Watch, cell phone, or computer with alarm function

Your Imagination

APPROX. TIME: 2 minutes, approximately 8 times per day

PURPOSE: To create a habit of viewing your life in intervals throughout the day. To practice this re-viewing, with no judgment, for the purpose of assessing if a thought or action is working in your life.

ACTION:

Option 1 - Set alarm to go off at least 8 times a day, in equal intervals, during your waking hours or:

Option 2 - Start exercise each time you go to the bathroom. For about 2 minutes, hit the rewind button on your imaginary video camera and review the interval between the last time you reviewed your 'life movie.' Use your mind to look at the last few hours as if it were a movie, with no judgment.

TONE: Fun and playful. Use movie metaphor as much as possible to view your day as if you were watching it on-screen

DEBRIEF: Is this thought or action working in my life? It is that simple. This need be your only question. Self-aware people live their lives deliberately and on purpose. They are awake and aware of their thoughts and actions most of the time. Knowing the LAW, that your thoughts create your life, does you no good if you do not pay attention to your thoughts.

TAKEAWAY: I will practice the exercise of Being The Observer until it becomes a habit in my life. This tool gives me the ability to assess my thoughts and actions. From that place I can create my life on purpose.

" The more you
are motivated by love,
the more fearless and free
your actions will be. "

– KATHERINE MANSFIELD

Creating a Judgment Free Zone

Your Thoughts Create Your Life...all the time. To know what you are thinking you learn to **Be the Observer** – to step back and view, with **No Judgment** your thoughts and actions.

Leslie – When I was growing up, I made up that I lived in a world full of judgment. When I say "I made up" I mean that we are making up our interpretation of the world all the time. There is rarely anything that is absolute because everyone has a slightly different perception. So to me, my actions, attitude, looks, thoughts were always being judged.

I noticed that, as a woman, I was often judged on how I looked. Looking good was very important in my family. As a woman, my hair needed to be "coiffed" and my face put together at all times. God forbid, I put on extra weight. Whenever I or another female relative in my family came home to Charlotte, the first comment was always about weight. "Why, Susie, aren't you the big girl now!" Of course Susie is 42 and, although once a size 8, she is hardly a double wide. Or, "why Lilly, you have finally lost that weight, sugar. You look so good." I'm not oblivi-

ous to the fact that most of us look better at a particular weight, but the comment was always about how you looked, not your health, career, or relationship.

There was also guilt. Guilt was used as a motivator, fear and last-ditch resort to get me to do just about anything. I don't know if people consciously use guilt, but I felt that it was in play a lot during my early years. When I was 25 and finally rebelled, I needed to create a way to live that did not include guilt and judgment. So, I left the church and became somewhat alienated from my mom. But I did not have a clue how to create a positive life. I was 40 before I started that path. What I have finally discovered is that fear, guilt, and judgment DO NOT motivate me. Now when I make a decision, it is not based on who will be mad or disappointed. It is made by my asking the simple question: "DOES THIS WORK for my life or DOES IT NOT WORK for my life?"

I live my life from a precept that nothing is wrong or bad. It either works for me or it doesn't. When you take away the negative energy of guilt, shame, fear, and judgment, and view things in the light of "this is working in my life or is not," then you can make a logical decision that is in alignment with your values and vision.

Whew, doesn't that feel better? The energy with which we look at situations is so critical. Mother Therese said, "If you have an anti-war rally I will not attend, if you have a rally for peace, then I'll be there."

Let's go back and look at judgment in another way. Many of us judge others by their appearance, race, gender, jobs, cars, and a score of other factors. We do much of our judging unconsciously and unfairly. We are not talking about using good judgment. We are talking about pre-judging, using criteria from past perceptions or learned prejudices when labeling others. Think back to your teen years. Do you remember all the cliques you had in high school? The jocks, nerds, cheerleaders, and band geeks? The ones who took shop, the ones who were all but invisible?

Some of those labels might make you smile, some might cause you to wince in pain and, more than likely, you know exactly where you fit. The deal about judging and labeling is that we take a major characteristic of a stereotype and decide that ALL those in that group are that way. We now know that all athletes are not stupid or cocky. But we may have decided to treat them that way. When we label someone, we never give them a chance to be anything other than their label. We never get a chance to know them for who they truly are. Now, you might say, "but we are not going to get to know everyone on a deep level." Yes, but when you label someone, even as you pass them in the hall at work, you are separating yourself from future possibilities.

As adults, we still judge. The groups just have new names. Below is a NOTICE in form of an email that Sean shared with me as we were writing this book.

Sean to Leslie – Wanted to share what I experienced this morning with judgment. I walked into the training room for the Day Trader course I'm taking. We all sat down and as they say in AA,

I started "taking everybody's inventory." First with the women—who was good-looking and who wasn't—then on to the men—who was smart and rich, and who was dumb and broke. I did all this before anyone started speaking. As we introduced ourselves, I actually started deciding who I could learn from and who I couldn't, after being in the room for one minute. What shocked me was how I judged them so quickly on so many different levels. I came up with five or more reasons to shut them out completely: race, sex, possible religion, education, and lack of charisma. I was in 100% judgment mode, and it was fast and automatic. Good Lord, I know better. I'm writing a book about this stuff. My observation is that either I'm doing this by habit at best, or I'm totally unconscious at worst. When I did NOTICE, which in fairness to me was within a few minutes, the actions I took to address my thoughts were: 1) I noticed it and decided that I wanted to stop, and 2) I talked myself out of it.

In my head I said, "Don't sit here and decide that you can't learn anything from this guy. Don't sell this guy short. YOU KNOW BETTER! Put yourself in his shoes and listen to what he's saying. Give him your full attention and stop making stuff up! Stop talking while he's talking and LISTEN!" It turns out he was laid off from his job due to a disability, and day trading is the way he is going to support his family. Instantly, I was filled with empathy, but if I hadn't shut up my thoughts, maybe I wouldn't have even heard him. So what could be lost on our reader is how the unconscious mind can and will judge on multiple levels at the same time in just a matter of seconds. You may not even realize you're doing it and you then have to scale this huge wall you have put up just to get back to the original place where you might connect, make a friend, or help yourself in some way.

This multi-level, lightning-fast judgment costs us more now than it did in the past. We live in a diverse, global community. If we are unconsciously searching for connection with people who only look, think, act, and talk the way we do, we are setting ourselves up to lose, personally and professionally.

As a side note, there are two salesmen in my company who refuse to run sales calls for Asians, Indians, or Muslims. I take these calls anytime I can .People can be so dense. We think we can hide our judgment, but we can't and we don't. We give ourselves away by not making cordial eye contact, and we assume that because we don't have a judging look on our face that the person we are judging doesn't know. They do know, and more importantly they FEEL it. In those first few minutes this morning, I am sure that my vibration in the room gave my thoughts away and maybe some even noticed the struggle on my face as I chastised myself.

I am simply in awe of the fact that a few years ago I would not have noticed the judgment and if I had I wouldn't have cared. Judging is what we do, I would have thought. I am not sure I would have the success in my business if I had not learned the concept of judgment-free zone and more importantly NOTICE. Thanks for letting me vent."

-Sean

In our opinion, if it wasn't for NOTICE, being the observer, we couldn't make any strides forward with our personal growth. When working with our coaching clients, a huge turning point happens when they NOTICE the judgment they have in their lives. They might judge the mates of their children, the co-worker who is foreign, and their next-door neighbor whose house just went into foreclosure. An application that you will learn in lesson 6 of this book, "Walking in Someone Else's Shoes," often shakes our clients to the core. Empathy is the most important of all human traits. It alone could change our world. Judgment always creates separation. Resolution, good business, and happiness cannot come about when we are separate.

When we are working with teens, we see the shift that happens when someone finally feels accepted and loved exactly as they are. They will grab the microphone and with an ease and grace of a seasoned professional, speak about their dreams and vision for the world. At a training in Dallas, a 16-year-old boy spoke on the mic at the graduation of the two-day workshop and told the adult audience that he had always thought it was so hokey when at beauty pageants people spoke of world peace. But that he had just spent the weekend with a mix of teens that represented a microcosm of the world (yes, he used the word "microcosm") and after two days, he was in love with every one of them. That he truly recognized that basically we were all the same and that by removing judgment we could create world peace. Did you hear that, people? This is a 16-year-old boy, who is very smart, but definitely in the "cool group," and he saw that this was possible with a group of teens—probably the most judgmental of all ages. Isn't it time that we adults held his hand and aided him in creating that world?

Leslie — JUDGMENT FREE ZONE

It makes no sense to me. I can understand not liking someone because they are mean or not wanting to hang out with someone because you have nothing in common. But I cannot for the life of me understand choosing to not like someone because of the color of their skin. This thought went through my head every day of 5th grade. This was the year of "integration" or, as we put it in my hometown of Charlotte, NC, simply "busing." I had gone to my neighborhood elementary school, Shamrock Gardens, until 4th grade and, the next year, I was bused to Plaza Road Elementary. It had been a completely black school (they didn't say African American back then) until 1970. I had not been raised to be prejudiced and no one in my family ever spoke poorly about blacks or called them names. So going to Plaza Road wasn't that big of a deal. It was even a little exciting. My mom was PTA president, and she was determined to make it the cleanest, nicest school in town. In fact, she was so upset with the condition of the buildings that she invited the school board to lunch at the school. They came, and in a couple of years, they tore down the old school and built a new one.

Well, maybe my Momma and I were ok with integration, but not everyone was. I remember regularly breaking up fights in the playground between blacks and whites. I was always the peace maker. It was in my blood.

By the time I got to high school, hanging out with people whose skin color was different from yours was not that big of a deal. Not totally, that is. Of course athletes of different colors would hang out together, and there were a handful of other groups, but dating? That was a big taboo. No one openly crossed that line in the mid-70s at my high school.

In 10th grade I was pretty innocent. I'd never been kissed and was basically a good Christian girl. Even though I had had boyfriends, I was pretty shy and didn't really know how to handle the attention I was getting. I had "gone with" a senior, "Mr. Garinger," the quarterback and president of the student body for a while, but I was so uncomfortable and shy, we didn't last that long. He hung out with the "cool guys" and one of them was awesome. He was one of the smartest seniors, a football player, and was voted best-looking in the school. He was BLACK, and we really liked each other.

We talked on the phone, passed notes, and would sit beside each other in the quad after lunch playing cards with a group of friends. But we never touched, dated, or crossed the lines that society said we shouldn't cross. Later in the year, one of my really good guy friends said to me, "Leslie, everybody knows what you are almost doing. If you don't stop soon, the white guys will never date you. You will be ruined."

I almost threw up. I felt so sick, disheartened, and furious that people could be so utterly stupid. He was the best catch in the school. His father was the president of a college. He was light years ahead of the other boys, and I did not have the courage to take a stand. I remember clearly how I slowly quit talking to him and passing notes, and I never told him why. It is one of the things I am most ashamed of in my life. I allowed other people's judgments to influence me so much that I turned my back on what I believed. I, the peacemaker in 5th grade, chose the path of least resistance and went along with the crowd.

In 2006, I was the trainer for the first Quest Teen Leadership training in Lake Village, AR, with a group of mostly African-American teens. It was the first of many. We would go on to train hundreds in that small town, along with many charter and alternative schools that were mostly African American. I was told then and many times since, "You're a middle-aged, white woman. Those kids are not going to listen to you." But they always did. They didn't judge. They may have for the first few minutes, but very quickly they would open up enough to hear the words and were wise enough to understand these universal truths. They accepted and loved me and knew that we are all more alike than we were different. Their acceptance has changed my life. Their acceptance has helped me forgive myself for the dishonor of my earlier actions. Judgment has no place in my life now or forever. It is my creed.

LESLIE OBSERVING

Voice of me at 16 if I had understood these concepts: "My actions aren't lining up with my beliefs....my actions aren't lining up with my beliefs.....this is why I feel so yucky. Justice—not judging others—this is the biggest part of me. When I take up for others I feel good about myself. When I don't do what my heart tells me I feel yucky. Got it: I hate feeling yucky. I love feeling proud of myself."

Now: When I am out of alignment with my beliefs, I feel it in my body. It is the BEING THE OBSERVER that makes me pay attention to my actions. Taking actions that make me feel this way Do Not Work for me. It is that simple. No need to feel guilt and shame. It just doesn't work. How different my life might have been if I had understood this tool at 16.

Sean — JUDGMENT FREE ZONE

Sept 26 2006 – message on MySpace

Sean,

You recently were sent a message by Erin in My Space. "Who the hell is this lady?" I am sure was the reaction you had, as she has not received any response from you. Here is the history: She has been my best friend since we were 12 years old and has been with me from day one of the journey that led me to you. My birth mother is Francyne Terry (Eubanks). Although I have had this information for many years, I found out just last year that she had a son in either 1978 or 1976. 99.99% chance that you are that son.

I tried contacting Frances in 1999 via mail. I did not get a response. This situation cannot be easy; as this may be the first time you have ever heard of me. But looking at your profile and knowing that you have traveled the world and are involved with children, I send this communication in hopes of you being compassionate enough to give her the message that I would like to speak with her.

I am a mother, so I know how difficult it was for her to make the decision that she made. I turned out ok - better than ok. So it needs to be said that I am not looking for a mother. However, I do have questions that need answers and I need to know my genetic health history. I will be 35 years old and I have an emptiness inside me that will not go away. The ball is in your court. Please respond somehow or someway. As an alternative you can email me at Alicia@aol.com. Thank you so much for your time and congratulations on all that you have accomplished in your life.

Alicia

•••

I have a sister, she's 35, and she is black! That's her picture! She's tall...and hot! I mean, she's not hot, she's my sister! What's wrong with me? Holy sh#t!! There's no doubt! She looks just like my mom! Does dad know? He's not the father. She cheated on him with a....wait....Does this mean that she slept with a..... That can't be! Oh God. This is going to ruin my parents' happy marriage. Dad will never take her back knowing she slept with a.....I've got to keep this a secret! He will be crushed. I can't call home! How would I ask my mom over the phone? I'll call grandma.

•••

Sept 27 2006 – message on MySpace

Hi Alicia,

You look just like my mom. My grandmother confirmed everything you shared in your message. I'll help you out anyway I can.

I would like to talk to you when you have a chance. Cell 214-000-0000 Office 972-000-0000...or leave your number and I'll call you. I look forward to visiting with you.

Sean

•••

She's my older sister and she's brilliant! She's tough, independent, a single mom, bullet proof, driven and educated! She got her degree from Columbia! She's funny, successful, and smart! She's....she's....ME. She is my flesh and blood. She is everything I love about my mother, and everything I thought my mother could be. All this time my mom had a black daughter. My heart breaks for you, Mom. I can't imagine how you felt every time a racist joke was told in your home and it reminded you of your daughter. If I had known, I would not have intentionally made comments to hurt you. I respect you and I love you. If I had known, I would have talked and acted completely different than I did. We are not only white. You are my mother and she is my sister. We are black and white. We will be better together than we were apart. You were too young to raise her and you chose adoption for her to have a chance to live a better life. I wish you hadn't hidden this from me, but wow, what a way to meet her! Glad MySpace was good for something! I can't help but wonder how my life would have been different had I known the whole time that I had a sister who was black. I respected all races who sacrificed themselves on the football field with me and trained in Karate with me, but I always saw myself as different when the games where over, not at all connected to them. I wasn't interested in crossing that line because I thought it didn't matter and it wasn't of any benefit to me. How could I have been so ignorant and judgmental then? I'm lucky now to have the chance to meet my beautiful sister!

SEAN OBSERVING

You can't really get a better gift than an unexpected sibling from a race that my family had openly jeered for years. Whatever judgments were so engrained from my family belief system were blown out of the water on that day. The pain I felt for my mom for the cruel remarks my dad had made over the years about blacks really had me re-think everything I had ever said or thought. How unconscious I was in this area of my life. If only I had learned to Be the Observer earlier.

Judgment Free Zone – Tool

Judgment always leads to separation. When we judge someone, we place them below or sometimes above ourselves. But it always leads to separation. When we judge ourselves we feel terrible. The main reason is that at our core we know that we are not bad. Maybe our actions or thoughts are not serving us, but judging ourselves keeps us separate from our TRUE selves. Judgment always leads to separation.

Judgment-Free Zone is a TOOL, not a law, because using it is a choice. It is imperative that you use this tool when you are Being the Observer. Viewing your life without judgment is key to being able to make choices that work for you versus choices that are determined by guilt.

EXERCISE: Judgment Free Zone

SUPPLIES: Phone, computer

APPROX. TIME: 1-3 minutes each for 3-10 times per exercise

PURPOSE: To connect with another in a way that will have you recognize we are more alike than we are different. Judgment is often a simple case of ignorance or not understanding. The more we understand the world consists of humans that are 99% the same as ourselves, we will hopefully choose compassion for one another.

ACTION: Choose a person to connect with for the exercise. Ask if they would be willing to play a game with you. The statement below can be shared in person, on phone, via text, or through email.

Say or write the statement "What you may not know about me is…" and then share something about yourself that the person does not know.

EXAMPLE: *I am an only child. I have a new puppy. I love to draw. I am scared to death of spiders. I never dance in public.*

Most people will respond with a similar type of statement. As the exercise progresses you will choose to share things that are more personal and intimate. Always start the exchange with "What you may not know about me is…

EXAMPLE: *I am going through a divorce. I just got laid off from my job. I am going to propose to my girlfriend. I've decided to go back to school.*

Doing this exercise in person is the best way to get the full impact. It is requested that you do not verbally comment on the statement shared by your partner. You may smile or nod or look empathetic, but the exercise is a practice in listening to another, not in consoling or fixing problems.

In actuality when you get to the more intimate statements you may feel led to share something similar, offer support, and just trust your instincts.

There is no specific amount of exchanges or duration of exchanges. As you get use to the flow of the exercise you may wish to set a certain number of statements when you begin with a new partner.

TONE: Fun and playful in the beginning; more serious when your statements become more intimate.

DEBRIEF: This exercise will allow the participants to recognize how much in common we have with other people. Whether you do this exercise with family, friends, co-workers or acquaintances it will create a connection that can change the dynamic of your relationship. Once you understand this dynamic, you don't even need to do the exercise with someone to know that they, like everyone, have a story. Empathy can be a natural choice. When you feel empathetic with another, it is impossible to judge.

TAKEAWAY: I can know at all times that regardless of race, socioeconomic differences, gender, sexual orientation, religion or cultural choices, as human beings we are more alike than we are different. I choose to see the commonality because judgment leads to separation and that does not serve anyone.

"Nothing ever happened
in the past that can
prevent you from being
present now; and if the
past cannot prevent **you**
from being present now,
what power does it have?"

– ECKHART TOLLE

LESSON FOUR

It's All Neutral

Your Thoughts Create Your Life...all the time. To know what you are thinking you learn to **Be the Observer** – to step back and view, with **No Judgment,** your thoughts and actions. Now that you can view an event or a thought, you have the ability to **Neutralize** it.

The lessons taught in this handbook are presented in a linear fashion, but they actually flow more in a circle or a spiral and can become a totally new way of living. We, the authors, of Think or Swim are left-brain personalities in that once we understood the concepts we needed a logical and systematic way to implement them into our lives. That is how the design of the 7 lessons came to be. If you believe in the law of attraction, and there are still things in your life that you desperately want and don't have, then there is a reason. Thinking positively about finding a new job when you have an underlying belief system that the world is out to get you will not work. You must go through the process of cleaning up your insides and change the beliefs that run you so that you create new ways of thinking.

Lesson 4 is truly amazing. The all Neutral concept in itself can do more to give you a joyful, peace-filled life than anything else. There were times that it literally saved our lives, as you will read in the stories we share in the book.

The explanation in a nutshell:

Take any object you see in a room and describe all the different things it might be. For instance, a chair can be a piece of wood or plastic, a desk, an umbrella, a shield, a weapon, or a stool. The list goes on. Let's move on to a baby. For some people a baby is a gift, to others it is a screaming annoyance, to still others it may be the end of a career or a life dream. What is it really? All objects, people, and events, are neutral until we decide what they mean to us. This is the true power of creating.

Let me explain with more detail. A chair, for instance, seems simple enough. You can describe what it is made of and you can list other uses it may have, but every person that views a chair will have a slightly different perception of the object. If you work on your feet you might think lovingly of how nice a chair would be for a short rest. If you are a 5-year-old, a chair may represent "time outs" and must be avoided at all costs. The chair is neutral. It is nothing, Play-Doh or a blank slate, until you decide to give it meaning with your perception.

When you look at the gear shift in a car there is Park, Reverse, Neutral and Drive. All of those gears represent movement or no movement except Neutral. In Neutral the car is waiting for you.

If our thoughts create our life and we learn to view our thoughts by being the observer (no judgment) then the next step is to make all the things we view (objects, people, and events) neutral. Then we take the reins of our life and decide what meaning all of these events will have for us.

Of course, you might say, making a chair neutral is pretty easy. What about events? That's where it gets tricky. Here is an example of an event that is neutral.

A man is driving to work one morning. He has on his best suit as he has a very important meeting with a potential new client. He is drinking a cup of coffee and suddenly a woman pulls in front of him and he slams on his breaks, spilling his coffee on his suit. The man calls his wife on his cell phone. "You are not going to believe what happened. This stupid woman driver pulled out in front of me. She didn't even look, and I have now spilled coffee all over my suit. Geez, I will never sign that new client looking like a slob with spilt coffee all over me." The man goes into his office and yells at everyone. He goes home after work fuming at his wife and kids that his day was ruined by a stupid woman driver.

A woman is putting her child in the car seat in the back of her car as she is rushing to get to work. Her cell phone rings and she answers it and begins to pull out of the driveway. She feels a bump and notices that her child is not in the back seat. Her son has snuck out of the car as she was talking, and she accidentally ran over him with the car. In a panic she grabs him, cradles him in her lap, and heads to the hospital.

The woman pulls in front of a car with a man who is drinking a cup of coffee headed to an important meeting.

This is an example of two different perceptions of the same event. The event is simply a car pulling in front of another car. The man chose to see the event that led to the spilling of his coffee as a catastrophe that ruined his day and, in turn, upset his employees and family. Had this man known what was happening for the woman in the car, it could have completely shaped his day in another way. He could have been sympathetic, never thought twice about the coffee, and told his new potential client how the coffee spill happened, demonstrating how caring he was, and maybe landed the job. Instead of showing up to the people in his life as a jerk he could have shown up as a compassionate man.

You might say to yourself, but he couldn't possibly have known what was going on in the car. EXACTLY! That is why it is neutral. You don't have to know, you can only know that your thoughts create your life in every moment and if you want to be a compassionate man, then you will take NEUTRAL events and create a perception that will have you be a compassionate man. Everybody has a story. You do not need to know the story to decide how you are going to perceive any event. There are so many nuances to this concept, but stick with me and let it soak in.

An extremely important piece of this concept is to understand that every event is NEUTRAL, waiting for you to give it life. There is no right or wrong to the perception you give the event. You will make the conscious, on-purpose decision, or interpretation of the event, in alignment with your beliefs and the vision of the person you want to be in the world.

People learning this concept often have some very intense reactions. In workshops, we have had people tell us that they were raped, and nobody was going to tell them that rape was a neutral event.

Leslie - I worked for many years in a sexual assault center in Atlanta and am particularly sensitive to this dynamic. My first words are to assure anyone that nobody has the right to force themselves on another, to touch or harm another, and in no way is making something neutral saying that the action is OK. Nevertheless, the event is neutral. When someone is raped they have the power to decide what the rape will mean for them. They may in the early days experience many emotions including rage, fear, sorrow, and despair. And whatever you choose to feel is perfectly ok. Time will go by and you will begin to create a feeling or perception of the event. For 99% of humanity this is an unconscious decision.

Typical responses might be:

- *I am never going to trust men again*
- *There is something wrong with me and no one will ever love me*
- *I must be very careful all the time or this will happen to me again*
- *Bad stuff always happens to me, I am scared all the time*

The gift of truly understanding neutral event is like the chair or like the spilled coffee, this too is neutral. You can decide whatever you want to decide about what the event will mean. You can decide to give NONE of your power to this man or event. You can choose to not let the event disrupt your life. You can choose that it was a moment in time and has no effect on who you are in the world and not to give it any power to disrupt the dreams you have for your life.

Practicing neutral event is key to consciously creating your life. It is a gift that sets you free from ever being the victim to anything or anybody. No one controls your thoughts, but you and your thoughts are what take a neutral event and make it something that supports you in having an amazing life.

Leslie — IT'S ALL NEUTRAL

I married the most wonderful man in the world, Joe Crow, on February 14, 2006. I was 46 and he was 50. We had both been married before. I had one grown child and he had two. We had been divorced for 7 and 15 years, respectively. We met each other at a study group in a church in Dallas. We were not looking for love. Isn't that, as all the poets say, when it shows up at your door? Nevertheless, Joe and I fell deeply in love. We began as friends, spending months getting to know each other, and as we opened our hearts, we began to realize that we were a perfect fit. As Forrest Gump says, we were like peas and carrots. Although we shared many similar beliefs and interests, we moved at different speeds. I tend to zoom and he was slow and methodical about everything. He could sit for hours and watch as a flower slowly unfurled, while I would answer emails, watch a movie, and talk on the phone all at the same time. But somehow it just worked. Our lives were filled with love and laughter and a sense of safety and peace I had never experienced.

On October 17, 2007, I got a call from a hospital in Dallas and was told that Joe was in the emergency room. Joe's son, Thomas, and my son, David, were both living with us at the time. Thomas worked for me with the Quest teen trainings and my son, David, worked for Joe in his roofing business. When I got the call, I grabbed Thomas and we got in the car as we called David and told him to meet us at the hospital. When we walked in they took us to a room with a social worker, a counselor, and the emergency room doctor. They started talking to us about a ladder that Joe was holding and about a burn in his hand and electricity. The doctor kept giving us these details until I asked him, "Are you going to tell me my husband is dead?" Of course I knew the answer. The look on their faces, the air that was sucked out of the room, the feeling in my head that I was under 20 feet of water—that was how I knew. And then time stopped. My life stopped.

Joe Crow was electrocuted as electricity from an overhead wire arced and hit the ladder he was holding as he was preparing to climb onto a roof. He died instantly.

I have experienced death and grief in my life, but there was nothing to prepare me for this. The pain blessedly came in waves. I now know why grief comes in waves because if the crest were to last for too long, we simply would not be able to stand it.

Was it a gift that my life was completely immersed in the teen workshops? All of our friends and family in Dallas were a part of this work. The 3,200 square-foot training facility was a mile from our home. I had just returned from Indianapolis and a teen training at a KIPP charter school. I was going to Arkansas in a couple of weeks to train more teens. Was this some kind of a sick joke? Did I spend every minute of my time and all of our financial resources on a program that told me that my husband's death was a neutral event?

And, yes, my precious husband's death was a neutral event. There was never a moment during those days or since that I have not known in every part of my being that his death was neutral. I lived the mantra that my thoughts create my life, and now was when the rubber would meet the road.

The funeral was one of the sweetest experiences of the affirmation of life I have ever known. Our lovely friends created a beautiful haven of flowers, candles, and food at the Quest training center for after the ceremony. Many of the teens from the workshops were there to show their love and support. One of them was a 16-year-old girl that had staffed many of the trainings over the past couple of years. She gave me a card and this is what she wrote,

"I know that you know that Joe's death is a neutral event and I know that right now you are choosing to be sad, and I know that in the future you will choose something else."

Can you believe that this incredibly gutsy young woman was telling me that my husband's death was a neutral event and on the day of his funeral? But as long as I live I don't think there will ever be another confirmation so pure that what we taught in our workshops had truly made a difference. For you see she got it! She understood exactly what it means for something to be neutral. It doesn't mean that you are a robot and that you feel nothing for the events of life. It means that you CHOOSE. We always CHOOSE. We are never victims to a circumstance; we CHOOSE what it will be for us. We CHOOSE how we will feel. We CHOOSE how we will live.

The night before Joe died, he, Thomas, David, and I watched the movie, "Fiddler on the Roof." We sang along with the music, we laughed, and we cried. Joe looked around the room at all of us and said, "It doesn't get any better than this!" Although he did not know that these would be among his last words, he was right: It doesn't get any better than this!

LESLIE OBSERVING

The gift of being able to understand literally in seconds that my reaction to Joe's death was completely my choice was a game changer for me. I had practiced neutralizing events for years and this was not the first tragedy since that time, but it was by far the biggest. I got to neutralize my thoughts almost hourly through the next year or two. It was probably what saved my life. If the event was neutral and I could choose any reaction, I decided I would consciously choose whatever would get me through the day. Some days it was escaping my grief by watching movies endlessly. Some days it was getting dressed and training teens in a workshop. Some days it was not leaving the bed. None of my choices were wrong. None of them were forced on me because of Joe's death. They were my choice, every day in every moment.

Sean — IT'S ALL NEUTRAL

"Watch this, Eric!" I threw a rock as hard as I could and looked over at my brother, who had ducked behind our makeshift bunker, to confirm that he could see I hit my target. Bingo! What a blast! This was as close to the shootout at the OK Corral as we were going to get. We were engaged in a good, old-fashioned rock war at the expense of all of the cars parked in the street that day. As we ducked behind the van in our driveway, I popped my head up to see the boys we were up against, and that's when I felt a thud. Barely conscious, all I could see was blood running down both sides of my face. I staggered back and forth and was now unable to see but could still feel the blood pouring out of my head. The world stopped and I could hear the commotion and I knew something hurt me. I was 5 years old, and I just had my forehead smashed in by an acme brick that was thrown by a teenager from across the street. It was a one-in-a-million shot, and it hit me dead in the center of my forehead.

The county hospital was understaffed that day, so my dad used a syringe full of water to clean the wound and pick the remaining pieces of brick & fragmented skull out of my hair as we waited for me to go into emergency surgery. I couldn't see my dad, but I knew he was there, I knew he was my doctor for now, I knew even at 5 that this hospital was terrible, but I was going to live. Six weeks later, I was released from Texas Children's Hospital with a full time helmet fixed to my head, chin strap, and all. I had options each day: I could wear a red one or a blue one, but I had to keep it on for 12 more months while my forehead healed. I shocked the doctors when we returned one year later to have a metal plate installed in my forehead. My skull had already grown back. It was official. I would be saved from the embarrassing explanation every time I passed through the metal detector at the airport, but that was the extent of the good news that day.

The doctors, in a very professional, studious way, set forth the parameters that I would be faced with for the rest of my life. They were the smart ones and we were to listen carefully as they predicted how my next 70 years would play out. Although I would not always be this cross-eyed, I would always have bad vision and would struggle with speech. I would be slower than the other kids academically due to the significant damage to my frontal lobe. I would need to attend special education classes and should not be expected to graduate high school. I would suffer from depression, extreme hyperactivity, and mood swings, and all of that would progress as I got older. Headaches and dizziness would be frequent and I would have to deal with that every day too. My hair would grow back, but the scar that runs from ear to ear across the top of my head would remain forever. Under no circumstances would I ever be able to participate in contact sports...ever. Luckily for me, I wasn't taking notes that day. Even better, I was too young to comprehend the instructions for how to live this new, limited life.

Here is a summary of the event: I was hit in the head with a brick by my neighbor. I had surgery to repair my head,

I went home, and I missed one year of school. Everything else that I decide to make up about my life based on this event is a choice. I hate to think of what my life would have been like if I had listened to the story the doctors told us that day. I would have missed the opportunity to be the captain of the Texas National Sport Karate Team, play college football, serve as the president of my fraternity, be the first in my immediate family to graduate from a university, start my own business, travel to over 40 countries, become a scuba diving instructor, start my own nonprofit organization, give a speech introducing a presidential candidate, write this book, or share this message with you.

APPLICATION
It's All Neutral – Law

This concept is a law. Everything is Neutral, but you get to choose whether to see it that way. This application is a tool to support you in the process. When you learn to look at events as being neutral, you are able to put any circumstance into perspective quickly. You will know how to identify limiting beliefs about yourself and the situation.

We talk about things that are "made up." These words speak to the fact that it is in our nature to invent limiting beliefs about ourselves and who we are based on an event in our lives. Until now, you may have used a single event that happened to you, such as losing your job, as an excuse to downgrade the opinion of what you are capable of, or even worse, WHO YOU ARE. Understanding this concept will do wonders for giving you peace and clarity. Practicing it will allow you to reinvent yourself, or depending on how you view it, get back to your original self. The opposite of this would be to "make up" a long, drawn-out story with a lot of drama and a resolution that doesn't serve you. The template provided will guide you to get clear on three things: Isolate the facts, become aware of what you made up about people and the world as a result of the event, and choose how you are going to move forward.

EXERCISE: It's All Neutral

SUPPLIES: Pen and paper; or a computer

APPROX. TIME: 10 minutes

PURPOSE: To learn how to take any event and neutralize it. Once that is done you can decide what it will mean for you. All events start out as neutral and those involved create their perspective of the event. We may have an instant reaction to a traumatic event, but we get to choose how we will respond and feel and what actions we will take. Neutralizing an event sets us up to be creators of our experience. We will never be a victim again.

ACTION: Using the story below as an example, take any event from your life and write about it with all the drama and pain you felt when it first occurred. Then follow the template to extract the facts. From that you can make up a "new story" of the event.

THE "STORY" OF THE EVENT:

"Just before I walked into Mr. Bell's office I saw Craig, the top producer, in the lounge and had to listen to him tell me how his production numbers are up this month. Mine would be too if I didn't live a balanced life and spend time taking care of my wife and kids. Mr. Bell, my boss, doesn't have a clue. I work my rear end off for this company. I've come in on weekends for the last two years and I do my part. But what do I get? A demotion, not a promotion! I always go above and beyond my job description. I'm ranked 25th out of 95 salesmen, but at least I'm here at work on time every day. Mr. Bell told me that there are going to be some changes and due to my recent drop off in sales, he wants me to move to the processing side. Why would I take a pay cut and go over there? I've been with this company for five years now and have one of the longest tenures of anyone. He should have told one of the new guys to do it. All I hear about is the cuts the company is having to make, but I have a family to support and sales is the best way to earn the income I deserve. We spent 30 minutes going over my accounts and I tried to explain how bad the leads are that I've been getting but he said, "All the leads were equally distributed." That's not true!! Craig has much better leads than me! But Mr. Bell didn't care what I had to say. He told me I could go to processing or take a severance package. I told him to keep his job and I would take the package and go where I would be appreciated.

Above is the "story." It may not have happened exactly like that but telling it in that manner gives you an excuse to FEEL the emotions of the event vs. OBSERVING the facts and coming up with a plan to move forward. Here is the template.

TEMPLATE:

THE FACTS ARE:

Facts about what happened (10 words or less per sentence)

1) I was called into Mr. Bells' office.

2) He said there were cut backs and offered two options.

3) I decided that I would take the severance pay.

WHAT I MADE UP ABOUT MYSELF WAS:

1) I was treated wrongly and should have been promoted.

2) I am not a good salesman.

3) I'm not a strong enough person to support my family.

4) My wife doesn't respect me.

5) My friends don't think I'm able to keep a job.

6) My kids don't look up to me.

7) I'll never find another job as good as this one.

8) I'm not smart enough to continue in sales.

9) I don't deserve to be rich.

10) I'm a failure and I'm not a real man.

11) I'll never be happy, loved, or respected again.

WHAT I MADE UP ABOUT THE WORLD:

1) Corporations are greedy and they don't care about people.

2) All of the good jobs are overseas and I have to make less money now as a result of global competition.

3) Companies aren't loyal to their employees and don't respect hard work.

4) This company was just waiting to replace me with someone younger.

5) The President and Congress don't care about little people like me.

6) The world respects a real man who can excel in sales.

WHAT I KNOW ABOUT WHAT HAPPENED WAS:

1) I am no longer employed with XYZ company.

WHAT I CHOOSE TO DO NEXT IS:

1) Hire a headhunter

2) Update my resume

3) Find another job

THE "NEW STORY" OF THE EVENT IS:

"I must admit I am kind of relieved. I really disliked my job and didn't want to have to work so much overtime. My family is the most important thing in the world to me. I will stop and breathe and get clarity on what I really want to do. I loved the part of my job where I got to spend time helping the customers. Maybe a 9-5 in customer service would be a better fit. Maybe this is an opportunity for a more suitable career move."

TONE: Deliberate and purposeful

DEBRIEF: This exercise will give you the ability to take the drama out of any event. You then get to choose its' meaning for you. We make up a story about everything. When we realize that WE are making up the story—that the event did not MAKE us do or think any particular thought—then we can make up whatever story we choose. This is how our THOUGHTS ARE CREATING OUR LIVES IN EVERY MOMENT. Life is not happening TO US. We are creating it from our thoughts.

TAKEAWAY: By using the tool, Be the Observer, and viewing, with No Judgment, the event, you will be able to extract the facts. Once you have the facts, you can create a new story that supports the life you want to create and the person you want to be.

" The credit belongs to the man
who is actually in the arena,
who strives valiantly;
who knows the great enthusiasms,
the great devotions, and
spends himself in a worthy cause,
who at the best, knows the triumph
of high achievement;
and who at the worst, if he fails,
...at least fails while daring greatly,
so that his place shall never be
with those cold and timid souls...
who know neither victory nor defeat. ,,

– THEODORE ROOSEVELT

Everything in Life is a Choice

Your Thoughts Create Your Life...all the time. To know what you are thinking you learn to **Be the Observer** – to step back and view, with **No Judgment**, your thoughts and actions. Now that you can view an event or a thought, you have the ability to **Neutralize** it and then **Choose** what it will be or mean to you.

Explanation in a nutshell:

Many of us go through life acting as a victim. We say we have no choice, that people are making us do things or feel certain ways or that we have to do things. As victims, we have no control—we let life happen to us and often blame other people for it. Go to work, pay taxes, wash the dishes, do homework, brush your teeth, breathe. All those things we HAVE to do, or do we? Do we really have to go to work? What happens if we don't? We get fired or end up on welfare or live with our parents, but we don't really have to work. If you will let this sink in you will realize that you don't HAVE TO do anything, but you CHOOSE to because you don't want to face the consequences, then in actuality you GET TO do it all.

While pondering the idea that everything in life is a choice, one frequently comes up against situations that seem to blatantly contradict this concept. Say a person has just gotten sick with the flu. They didn't choose the flu. Within this last sentence is the key to understanding the idea that everything is a choice. The act of choosing is by definition momentary. It is impossible to choose to do something in the future, because the actual decision lies in some future point where the action is taken. Decisions can only be made simultaneously with the action that brings the desired result. If a person chooses to take a trip, they only really decide the moment they step foot onto the boat. The supposed decision-making taking place in the mind prior to the action is valueless because it is constantly subject to change. At any point, a person can change their mind. The person can also decide what they are thinking at any given moment, further emphasizing the proposal that everything is a choice, even one's thoughts. Immediately, one can either think about the color red or the color yellow, about death or about birth. Now back to the person with the flu. It is impossible for them to revisit the past and prevent the flu. However, their choices during the moment of illness are limitless. They could take actions and choose mindsets that would lead to feeling worse both physically and mentally. Conversely, the person could take as much rest as possible, equate the time in bed with an opportunity for general reflection, visualize and focus on being healthy, and work determinedly towards wellness (fluids, diet, medicine, etc.) in order to accelerate his/her recovery. One does not choose the flu. One chooses to fight the flu. "Everything in life is a choice."

We remember the first time we heard the statement that everyone was 100% responsible for their lives and we thought, "Well, sure we are, no one is the boss of me!" But as we become very conscious of being self-aware, we began to notice our words and how we react to circumstances in our life. We might not gripe about our jobs anymore, because we work for ourselves, but we might be critical of our employees' performances. We might act like a victim because we won't take the time to train them or take other appropriate action. So, wait a minute. If we are 100% responsible for our lives, then we are responsible for ALL the reactions we have to ALL the events that surround our every waking moment. Wow, if we are going to be self-aware people who own that we create our lives from our thoughts in every moment, then, darn it, we are going to need to be awake and conscious all the time. Was this going to be too hard? Could anyone possibly be really "conscious" all the time? After years of living these lessons, we can tell you that we are not in any way conscious 100% of the time. But it is now such a part of our lives that when we get into "victim mode" we catch ourselves much more quickly. Now, when we NOTICE that we have slipped into unconscious mode we can instantly shift from blame to ownership.

Leslie - About a year ago I spent three weeks as a vegan. I lost a few pounds and physically felt great, but it literally took up hours of my day. Any time I was hungry, I had to really think about what I could eat. I had to plan ahead as fast-food restaurants were not a viable choice. I read books and bought vegan magazines, and it was on my mind almost every moment. In the fourth week, I took a consulting project and I was working about 12 hours a day. Well into that week, I was starving and someone ordered a cheesy, pepperoni pizza. It was all she wrote.

I have friends who have been vegans for years. It's no big deal. They aren't tempted. They don't go hungry. It is a way of life. Just as any other practice such as yoga or running, it becomes a part of your life and you simply desire to live this way more than not. Living your life as a conscious, awake person is a practice that becomes easier as time goes by. But there is one difference concerning these lessons compared to other practices. Once you wake up, once you understand the ability to be self-aware—to be the observer—we believe it is impossible to completely go back to sleep or be unconscious again.

We often joke with our clients and workshop participants that once they wake up they can never really go back to sleep again. For example, imagine understanding that you really don't have to go to that job that you hate. You DON'T have to go to work there ever again. Wow, let that sink in for a minute. So you hate your job. You could quit. Ok, you have bills and you say "I can't quit." Baloney! You and I both know you can quit. You don't because the pain of going to work is less than the pain of not having the money to pay the bills. Going to work is less painful than looking for another job. Whoa. All of a sudden you have no one to blame. When you wake up to this concept, as you are waking up to all the others, you realize that you are the only one creating your life and, darn it, there is no one to blame for your life but yourself.

We had a workshop in a school in Texas and one of the students' moms called the principal to complain about the workshop. Fortunately the principal had been in attendance so knew the context of everything that was taught. The mom said, "My son came home yesterday and I asked him to take out the garbage. He said that he had learned that he didn't HAVE to do anything, but that he GETS to." The mom went on to rant for the next few minutes on the nerve of her son telling her that he didn't have to do anything. The principal said, "Did he take out the garbage?" The mom replied, "Uh, yes." "Well, what's the problem?" the principal asked, with a smile on her face.

How many times have we said to our kids, "Change your attitude," or had our boss say to us, "If you had a better attitude you might have gotten that promotion?" The difference in what they are saying and what we are teaching is this: Whether you have a BAD or a GOOD attitude doesn't matter. Just OWN that YOU are CHOOSING it.

When it comes to choice, another tool that helps is knowing that most choices we make come from one of two places, a place of Love or a place of Fear. An example is that I have been offered a promotion at work, but I must move to another city if I take the job. So I NOTICE, I observe how I feel about this move. Am I fearful of change? Am I worried I won't be able to handle the responsibility? And do I think in any way that I am not worthy of this promotion?

When making choices like this, our only job is to pay attention to our bodies, our meter for our intuition, and how we feel when we are making a choice. Love feels warm, relaxing and creates an openness in the center of your body around the heart area. Fear feels cold, like a contraction. It's that tight feeling in your chest or the knot in your stomach. When we become attuned to our body, our intuition, and learn to listen to its' messages, we can quickly notice if we are in a place of love or fear.

Leslie — **EVERYTHING IN LIFE IS A CHOICE**

I bought the brown leather couch and the three-year warranty because of the tar and the ink. Joe always had something on his clothes: tar, food, or ink from a leaky pen. It was a family joke, and I remember sharing it from the pulpit when I spoke at his funeral. I shared it as one of the "52 things I love about Joe Crow" that I had written for him on his 52nd birthday. Of course I didn't know that his 52nd birthday would be his last.

But in August of 2008 for a day, actually almost a whole week, I had hardly left the couch at all. I couldn't make myself leave the house. How could the pain still be so deep? The phrase, "cuts you like a knife," is so dead on. It had been 10 months and I could not get out of this hole that is the brown leather couch. "I'm a freaking trainer of transformation. A guru of 'Be the Change.' 'Your thoughts create your life.' Buck up sister and get off the darn couch."

"I've got to have some help! God, you have got to help me." I had reached a point where I didn't think I could go on. I was close to considering what it would be like not to feel the pain, anymore. I had never been tempted to commit suicide before, but then it seemed like a better alternative than living with the pain.

"It's time for me to move forward. I've got to make a living. I've got to connect with people. I've got to get off this couch." I cried for hours. I cried for days, and at the depths of despair, the prayer I prayed to God was, "Let me feel joy again. I must feel joy. I can't keep living without the feeling of hope and joy."

Nothing happened immediately. I guess at some point I got dressed, left the house and continued living. But soon after that day I got an email.

Prior to the email, a few months earlier, I had reconnected with a girlfriend from high school. She still lived in Charlotte, and we were catching up on our years apart. Carol loved teens and when I shared the Quest program with her, she decided to bring her daughter to Dallas to participate in a teen training. She also told me that we were having our 30-year high school reunion in September and encouraged me to go. I had moved away from Charlotte after high school and hadn't seen my friends since the 10-year reunion. Reconnecting with my old friends would be really good for me and maybe just the impetus I needed to move forward with my life.

I was registered on classmates.com and I noticed that someone had sent me a note. All it said was, "Are you going?" It was signed Joe Cude. When I first read it, my heart stopped. All I saw was Joe. My husband's name was Joe Crow. It was so surreal to get an email from someone who had the same first name, the same last initial, the same number of letters in the name. It was like a sign, a message.

Joe Cude was my best guy friend in high school, but we always called him Joey. We had gone to the same elementary school, lived in the same neighborhood, and had been raised in the same middle class, polite southern manner. Although he and I were just friends and never dated, we always liked each other in that other way. During high school we use to talk on the phone for hours. He was the good-looking athlete, the cool dude with a really big heart, and when I saw his email, I remembered how much I had missed him over the past 30 years.

We had a blast at the reunion and sat in the parking lot until 4 a.m., catching up on the past 30 years. He had gone through a very messy divorce and really needed someone to talk to who could bring a different perspective. I shared about Joe, our life, and the pain I could not get past. Joey listened and understood.

I returned to Dallas and we continued to talk for hours on the phone every day.

I had been thinking about moving to Charlotte after I reconnected with my girlfriend Carol, but this new friendship with Joey cinched the deal, and by Christmas, I was a North Carolina resident again. Joey picked me up at the airport, and we drove to the mountains for our first official date. When we pulled into the parking lot of a restaurant, the letters on the license plate of the car in front of us were JOY. For me that was a sign. God had literally answered my prayer. Not only did he give me Joy, he gave me a gift that would heal my heart, my old friend Joey. After a year of unbelievable sadness and the loss of the desire to live, I chose life and I chose joy.

LESLIE OBSERVING

The ability to observe my reactions to Joe's death was just and only that—the ability to observe, to NOTICE. What I did with that notice was completely up to me. It would be crazy to think that making an event neutral means you don't feel anything. You would be inhuman to not feel pain from a loved one's death. The understanding is that I am not a victim or a "poor pitiful me" because my husband died. Joe's death is neutral. The CHOICE for me is how I will choose to live. The choice to be sad was a perfect decision until it no longer worked. Being on the brown leather couch no longer worked.

Reconnecting with Joey was such a gift. I will admit I have had moments of feeling guilty that I could be happy again. But I also know that Joe would want me to be happy. As I have said before, I want guilt to have no place in my life, and it is my CHOICE to embrace love and life again.

Sean — EVERYTHING IN LIFE IS A CHOICE

In 1984, at age 8, I was a green belt in karate and competing every weekend in a different city all over the state of Texas. Our family would load up in our van, and dad would drive us all over. It was like every weekend was a vacation, and my older brother, Eric, and I were kicking butt, so we all had fun. My brother and I trained hard, excelled, and were both ranked in the top 10 in Texas. The local newspapers ran a picture of us surrounded by all of our trophies, looking tough like Karate Kids would.

As we got older, we were two of just three kids to ever earn a brown belt in our martial arts system under the age of 16. We were leaders in the dojo and often were asked to be assistant instructors in classes with lower-ranked students. That was the highest honor and now, as junior brown belts, with this recognition and new responsibility, our karate lives couldn't get any better. We would have to wait until we were 16 to test for our black belts, but after that, the sky was the limit. Martial arts was a great outlet to release our abundant energy, to learn to focus, and to stay busy doing something really fun, healthy, and productive. We kept training, and we kept winning tournaments.

One day as our Dad was taking us to class there was a note posted on the door from Sensei Jim that said the school was closed. We peeked through the window to see for ourselves that the building was empty. What had happened? Was it over? No more karate? My brother and I were devastated, and over the next few weeks, our Dad tried to find us another dojo. Everybody knew who the best instructors in Texas were and we narrowed it down quickly to Al Garza's American Karate Club. He had the largest competition team and, although we beat them on a regular basis, he was the best and his students won the most overall. I admired the way they all showed up together as a team to compete and supported each other. His kids were tough, and I loved watching Mr. Garza fight, as he was fast and was always handling opponents who were much bigger than himself. We asked to join Mr. Garza's school and although he accepted us, he asked that we start over at no-belt status.

Since we were already brown belts in another style, he promised to advance us quickly through the beginning belts as we earned it. My brother and I were faced with a choice that was a huge shot to our egos. Yes, we had egos at 11 and 13 years old. "Start over as a no belt? Not even a white belt? We kick these kids' butts all the time! We just had our dojo closed or we wouldn't even be here. I deserve to come in here as a brown belt. Let me spar any of your brown belts my age and if they can beat me and my brother, well, then we'll start over as no belts, but otherwise we'd appreciate a little respect here. We were a bit like Jack Nicholson in the movie, "A Few Good Men:" "I'd rather you said, 'Thank you,' and let me on my way!"

The conversation in my head for the first few months of class was, "I hate this. I'm a better fighter than most of these students, and I'm embarrassed to hold such a low rank when I was once a brown belt. I'm making friends here, but most of these kids don't like me because I'm better than them, and I'll kick their butts if they have a problem with how hard I like to hit them when I spar. I don't like these instructors. I'm being promoted quickly, but I miss Sensei Jim, and I miss training with my brother."

My brother had quit. This was a huge choice in his life and had a huge effect on mine. He decided that it was too much to be stripped of his rank and he had too much pride to join forces with a rival school. I understood and I wanted to quit, too, every day. But I chose to go to karate class 5 to 6 days per week and stick it out. I wasn't happy about it and I missed hanging out with my brother, but I chose to go for it.

I loved martial arts. I was a natural and I loved to compete. I set the goal to be a black belt in four years and that was what I would focus on. The decision not to quit proved to be a life-changing event that would shape me and put me on the path of a successful and rewarding life. I chose every day not to quit until it became a habit. Within a year, I was thriving. My best friends were in karate, we traveled together. Our families were the best of friends and, looking back, it was the best of times.

Three and a half years later, at 15, I tested for my black belt. It was the greatest accomplishment of my young life, and I know now that it also saved my life. The test was 14 hours long. Most of it was behind closed doors, and I consider that test to be the hardest thing I've ever done. My brother was there as a spectator for the last few hours and saw the mandatory 12 rounds of sparring at the end. He was proud of me, my parents were proud of me, I WAS PROUD OF ME, and Master Garza reported, "There has been a new standard set in black belt testing by Sean Eubanks." That was the highest compliment anyone could receive from Master Garza at the time, and I was honored to be compared to such an elite group of people. When he tied that black belt around my waist, I knew I had done something HUGE. I didn't realize how huge.

Before I was finished training at his dojo, I had achieved a #1 ranking in fighting in the state of Texas, and the number #2 ranking in all of North America. Most important, I made great friends, achieved good enough grades to get into college, and had a clear path to where my life was going next. Master Garza helped me maximize my potential, took me from being good to being great, and made me a true champion. I continued to train and worked as an assistant instructor at his school.

Two years later, I went to college and my brother went to prison. There is no doubt in my mind that my brother's decision to leave karate was the deciding factor for the path that his life has traveled. My choice to put one foot in front of the other and stay committed to training at Master Garza's dojo continues to reward me to this day. His message of respect, discipline, commitment, perseverance, humility, achievement, positive mental attitude, and being humble before God was the reinforcement of what my parents wanted for me. At the time, as a teenager, I was unwilling to learn it from them. He led by example, and today has hundreds of black belts who live happy and successful lives. He probably would downplay his role in their success, but

I want to be clear that choosing to train at his dojo saved my life. What I also learned from him was how to lead by example. He practices what he preaches, and he loves what he does for a living. That example in itself is huge for me as I lead in my own business and seek to do what I love to do. My choice to continue to train in the martial arts led me to start my own nonprofit organization and help share the gifts and opportunities I enjoyed as a young martial artist.

After a presentation of my program to a karate school in Dallas, a friend in the martial arts thought enough of what I was doing to introduce me to Leslie Palmer, the co author of this book, and creator of the teen workshops. Leslie and I met on a Wednesday and, by Friday I was staffing a teen training. That training led to more trainings, and as life would have it, the opportunity to test these concepts in this book against real-life challenges. I did and they worked. From that point forward, I was hooked on the concepts. I continued to apply them to my life and knew I wanted to share them with the world.

SEAN OBSERVING

It is easy to see from the example of this story that everything is a choice and that our choices create our lives. The example of my brother choosing one path and my choosing another is an extreme example of choice and consequence. As a child, I did not see my opportunity to start with no belt as a "get to," but eventually my attitude changed. I honor that time in my life as a huge learning experience and am so grateful that my inner guidance had me choose to stay.

Every day of my life is a Get To. It is my nature to grab life with gusto, but it was a learned trait to see all of life's challenges as a gift—a Get To.

Everything in Life is a Choice – Law

Everything in Life is a Choice is a LAW. It is an indisputable fact, but choosing to use the tool in the application below is totally a choice. Understanding this concept and living it every day is like flying. I am free to do anything I choose at any time. Of course you have got to REALLY understand it at your core to see life in this manner. But this is what puts a spring in the step of us Think or Swim people. When a choice has to be made, all you have to do is THINK, "What will serve my life the most and align with my beliefs?" and then do it with GUSTO. If it is not an obvious choice, listen to your body and decide. Which choice is from LOVE and not fear?

It gets pretty easy after you live this way for a while. The exercise below will help you see just how easy it can be.

EXERCISE: Everything in Life is a Choice

SUPPLIES: Pen and paper

APPROX. TIME: 5-7 minutes

PURPOSE: Once you learn that there is nothing in life that you HAVE to do then you can accept that everything in life is a GET to. It really is a choice. If you are choosing to do something then choose a good attitude to accompany the action.

ACTION: At the top of a piece of paper write HAVE TO, and then list all of the things that you hate to do. Have fun with it. Let your list include things like chores, visiting in-laws, paying taxes, going to work, shaving, etc.

When you have written at least 20 items, go down the list and ask these questions for each item:

- Do I have to do this?
- What will happen if I don't?

Play out the scenario of what happens if you choose not to do it. At that point you can really decide. Hey, I don't really HAVE to do this. Or you might say, if I don't do this, I will have heck to pay. If you don't really have to do the item then you will know that you are CHOOSING to do it. Draw a line through each item you don't have to do and beside it write GET TO.

TONE: Fun and light

DEBRIEF: Once you have done this exercise, you realize that there is NOTHING that you have to do. It is always a choice. Change the verbiage in your every day speech to GET TO. You can say "I get to go to work," or "I get to clean the house," and notice the looks you get from your friends.

TAKEAWAY: Everything in life is a GET TO. You are never a victim. Everything is a choice.

" An eye for an eye
only ends up making
the whole world blind. „

– MOHANDAS GANDHI

Forgiveness = Freedom

Your Thoughts Create Your Life...all the time. To know what you are thinking you learn to **Be the Observer** – to step back and view, with **No Judgment**, your thoughts and actions. Now that you can view an event or a thought, you have the ability to **Neutralize** it and then **Choose** what it will be or mean to you; to lighten the load, choose **Freedom through Forgiveness**.

Most religions teach forgiveness. When Peter asked Jesus how many times should we forgive he said 70 times seven. But do we really know what Jesus meant in that statement? Did he mean that if our neighbor steals from us every day that we continue to forgive until we reach the 491st time? We understand the underlying message that there is no limit. That forgiveness isn't about being passive and letting people abuse you. It is about letting go and moving forward.

For most events, we can learn to practice letting go. Someone breaks in front of you in traffic. NEUTRALIZE (dude could be in a real hurry) and CHOOSE to let go. That is a practice and is simple enough to incorporate into your everyday life, but what about the big events? What about rape? What about murder? In the bestselling book, *The Shack*, the main character deals with the pain of his daughter being murdered in an extremely brutal way. He cannot forgive. The issue is not so much forgiving the murderer, but forgiving God.

Let's look at forgiveness in a new light:

Forgiveness is not about exonerating the person or nullifying the event that has happened to cause you frustration, anger, embarrassment, or pain.

Forgiveness is about letting go, cutting the umbilical cord that holds you to the past—whether the past is years, weeks, days, or moments ago.

Forgiveness understands that the past will never be any different. It is about freeing yourself from the burden of carrying around anger, frustration, and pain.

Forgiveness is about living a life full of joy, love, and acceptance. It is about FREEDOM.

If we did not practice these lessons in our everyday lives, neither of us is sure we could have made it to today. There is not one ounce of our beings that doesn't believe completely that our thoughts create our lives. That by practicing the art of witnessing your life, with no judgment, you can choose to neutralize any event. That you can choose how you want to perceive the event and how you want to live your life. But wow, the BIG ones? What about the really big ones? What about the events that send our lives down a completely different path? Down a road that we had never planned on going?

It is sometimes easier to look at someone else's experience and guide them to forgiveness. Let us share an example from one of our workshops where Leslie was the lead trainer.

Juan was a young Hispanic boy that lived outside of Dallas. He had a loving family and lived in the same neighborhood as his best friend, Miguel. These two boys had been friends since third grade. They were together all the time and they both loved cars. Juan and Miguel already had their lives planned out. They would open a garage together, fix cars, build their own hot rods, and live in the same neighborhood for the rest of their lives. Juan and Miguel were in eighth grade and, one day after school, as they were walking home, they reached the corner. Juan continued and Miguel turned to go down the adjoining street to his house. "Come over after dinner and we'll look at this new car magazine I got," said Juan. "Will do, man." As Juan continued on his way home, he heard a shot. The sound came from the street around the corner. "Miguel!" yelled Juan, as he turned and ran as fast as he could. Miguel was a lump in the sidewalk. He was lying in a pool of blood after having been shot three times. He was dead before Juan could get to him.

Four months later, Juan's mother dragged him to a Quest teen training. When it was time for the kids to come into the training room, Juan would not stand up. His mother was on the floor crying and begging him to go in. "Please make him go in the training, Miss Leslie." "I can't, honey. That's not how Quest works," I said, as I turned to the young man. "Juan, here is the deal. I am going to ask every person in the room to listen to me for just 30 minutes. I will explain the training and what you will learn and what is expected. If you decide to stay, you will have to stand in front of the room, make eye contact with me, and commit to stay for the entire 19-hour, 2-day training. The only way this program will work is if you CHOOSE to stay. So all I ask now is for you to give me 30 minutes. If you want to leave, no one will be mad at you. All I ask is for 30 minutes. Can you give me that?"

Juan would hardly lift his head but he finally said, "All right." With that, his mom was laughing and crying and hugging him as she pushed him in the door.

"Everything in life is a choice—everything. What if I could show you in the next 19 hours that you are totally creating your life with your thoughts? That no one controls your thoughts but you. That means that you and only you are 100% responsible for your life. That you can learn how to intentionally, on purpose, create any life you want to have. That you have everything you need right now inside of you to make this life happen."

Every training begins the same way with 40 teens sitting

in chairs with their arms crossed, looking at the trainer with a mix of loathing, boredom, fear or "I-would-rather-die-than-be-here" looks on their faces. As the trainer I always say the same thing. Give me 30 minutes. Somehow, they are intrigued enough to choose to stay.

On that particular weekend, as the teens were lined up to make their commitment to the training, I saw Juan inch forward. When he got to me, I lifted his chin and held his eyes with mine. "Are you in, Juan? Do you commit? Will you do whatever it takes?" "Yes, Miss Leslie." It was all I needed to hear. At that moment I knew that Juan would receive the healing he needed to move forward. He just needed to believe enough in himself to take a chance.

On the second day of the workshop, we begin the day with the exercise, "Everybody has a story." The adult staffers in the room, who might be volunteers or teachers, when we are in a school, sit at the front of the arc of chairs and share stories from their teen years. The students in the room are riveted. I have experienced this exercise with thousands of teens, and it is always the same. The adults share from their hearts the circumstances of their teen years. They are open and vulnerable, and you can see the look of amazement on the faces of these kids. Everybody has a story. The principal of their school might share that she had a baby at the age of 16 but decided to continue her education. Their stuffy older math teacher might share that his father was an alcoholic, and he was always too afraid to have friends come over, as his dad might embarrass him. All of the teens can relate to one or more of the adults. Everybody has a story.

The reason for sharing the story is always the same: We are way more alike than we are different. Regardless of circumstances, our lives at 16, or 30, or 50 are our creation. Nothing is so big that we cannot get past it and move on. After we all share our stories, I will explain the true meaning of forgiveness. It is NEVER about exonerating or letting off the hook the person that has hurt you. It is KNOWING that the past will never be any different. It is taking back any power that you have given to the event. It is about choosing.

Juan shared his story. It was hard for him to speak through his tears. Every young man in that room had been told in their life that crying was not cool. Boys don't cry. Today it did not matter. There were no dry eyes, whether they were the girls', the boys', or the teachers'. Juan shook as he expressed the pain and frustration that he could not save his friend. "Why wasn't it me? Why didn't I walk with him to his house that day? I would have seen the car, I would have protected him."

"I can't forgive his killer. I can't and I won't."

Juan's mother had shared with me that he was beginning to drink and use drugs. There was a gang in the area that had been courting him. She knew that she was about to lose her son to the streets.

I knew all of this as I knelt down in front of him. I knew

that my words might have some effect on his life and that they might have none at all. All I knew at that moment was that he could be my boy and I would do whatever it took to show him there was a way to freedom.

"Juan, if you continue to hate, if you continue to drink and use drugs, if you continue down this path, you will NEVER have that garage you and Miguel planned. THEY will win."

Every day that goes by when you don't thrive, when you choose not to love, not to be happy, you are giving all your power to Miguel's murderer. He wins. You cannot let him win."

"All this anger is like a hot fire, burning in your belly. It's a cord that is connecting you to the killer. You are forever connected to him unless you choose to cut that cord. The word forgiveness simply represents a knife, a knife that you can use to cut that cord that connects you to Miguel's killer. Get rid of him. Get rid of that hatred that binds you to him. Let it go. Choose to live. It is what Miguel would want."

Is it possible to be healed in a moment, to forgive and release and move forward? Yes, absolutely. But for most of us it is a letting go and then a picking back up, and letting go and then picking back up again. But knowing, being awake, being the witness, understanding that what you are thinking will create your life. That gift makes the picking up happen less and the letting go happen quicker. It's all a choice.

Leslie — **FORGIVENESS=FREEDOM**

Everybody has a story.

This is the story I share in every teen training:

My dad never wanted me. My mom wanted me more than anything in the world. I guess that should balance things out, but it never really did. I am about eight years old when I start to understand that my home is very different from others. I live with my grandmother and mom. I am loved and happy and life is pretty good. But about once every two or three weeks, my dad comes to town. I hate it, because I have to stop playing with my friends and take a bath and get dressed up. My mom and I go to pick him up at the airport. Not at the main terminal, but at the private terminal because my dad has his own private plane. It is a twin-engine Cessna, and he flies it himself. I know this is pretty cool, but I am eight, and I don't have a lot of life experience so I don't pay it much attention.

The day usually goes like this. I hug him, he gets in our car, and all three of us go to a restaurant for lunch. We then take him to a hotel, and we might hang out in his room for a while. He gives my mom some money for food and expenses, and then we go home.

I always feel very awkward. It is like he is a stranger that I am supposed to love. He kisses me and tells me he loves me, but it is just weird and I am never alone with him, which is good because I am very shy and don't know what to say to him, anyway.

This is not how dads on TV act, and he is not like the fathers of my friends.

As I get a little older, I begin to "make up a story" about my life. In hindsight, I can see clearly that there were a set of circumstances that were all neutral and that I gave them an interpretation that formed my life. But I didn't have the advantage of understanding these lessons, so as a young girl and as a teenager I only saw one thing.

My dad didn't want me and that must mean there was something wrong with me.

"How could he not love me? I am the perfect little girl. I am sweet, nice, and pretty cute. I never break the rules. I am smart. My teachers like me. I go to church, pray, and read the bible. Why doesn't he want me? He doesn't have any other children to take any of his time. Also, he is very rich. He has several houses, a farm with horses, beach houses, a boat, a motorcycle, several cars, and, of course, his own plane. Surely he would be proud to have a nice, little girl in his life." These are the thoughts that went through my head much of the time.

But the truth was, only a few people in his life even knew about me. Most of his family and friends didn't know I existed until I was 16. He died when I was 32 and my son was 11 years old and when we sat in the family section at the funeral, people came up and said, "Well, I never even knew Craig had a child."

Everybody has a story, and this part of my story has probably done more to create the woman I am today than any other factor.

In my mind, if the man described above who was my father did not want to acknowledge me then I must be something to be ashamed of. This interpretation could have had me go in many different directions. I could have chosen a "screw-you" attitude, partied and gone wild. I could have said, "I will show you," and turned my back on him completely. But instead I decided I would be perfect. I don't know how many of you have tried that path, but it is a killer. I would be perfect. I would do what God and my mom told me to do. I wouldn't drink, do drugs, have sex, or cuss. I would obey all the rules and make sure everybody (if not my dad) loved me.

This is a really hard road, and I know that marrying at the age of 19 to someone who would take me to Germany was an escape. Maybe this guy would love me, and when that marriage didn't work, at 26, I married the very next guy I dated. Maybe this guy would love me.

At the age of 40, I realized that none of "the story" was true. I had "made up" that my dad didn't want me, that my dad was ashamed of me. Because this was the interpretation I gave this neutral event, I became a person who strove to be good enough for someone to love. I could have made up a completely different story. I could have taken that neutral event and decided, "Wow, my father is an extremely smart and successful man. Even though he is crazy busy, he chooses to visit me. I must be pretty amazing to have come from such a pretty mom and such a smart dad. He is willing to pay for my college education, give me cars, and help me with other expenses. I am going to follow in his footsteps, start my own business, and have a home at the beach."

Does it matter which story is true? Can anyone really say what perception is the truth? We decide the perception or "the story" we are going to create from the neutral event by the intention we have for our life. It was not until I reached the age of 40 and truly forgave him and began to consciously create my life that I found true peace.

I now have made up a different story. My father did the best he could at the time. He had an eighth-grade education because he dropped out of school when his father died to take care of his many brothers and sisters who were still at home. He worked hard every day of his life and was truly brilliant. He created a company that went public when he was 39 years old, and he employed hundreds and supported many members of his family. My dad was afraid to trust. My dad was afraid to love. He never really had a home or a family of his own. He drank a fifth of liquor almost every night of his life. On his death bed, he told me to always work and that money would never make me happy. He told me a few days before he died, "I loved you as much as I could." At the age of 40, I decided that was good enough for me.

Forgiveness = Freedom for me is not about forgiving my father. It is about me letting go of the story I made up about a neutral event. It is about letting go of the thought that I'm not good enough to be loved. When I forgave and let go of all the pain and anger, I was able to truly love myself. By changing my thoughts about myself, I was able to attract two wonderful, loving men into my life. Both of them named "Joe." I do not believe that I would have found that kind of love had I not healed the pain I had created from the relationship with my dad. What if I had understood this when I was a teenager? How might my journey have been different?

I use to think that I created the teen trainings for my son as I wished he had had the opportunity to learn these lessons earlier in his life. But a good friend had me see that I really created them for myself. My life path has given me the examples to design this formula for living and what a gift these lessons were at 40, but, oh, the gift they would have been at 16.

LESLIE OBSERVING

Although I shared much of what I learned from this experience in my story, what BEING THE OBSERVER could have done for me in my youth would have been so huge. My father died before I had any understanding of self-awareness or the true meaning of forgiveness. If I could have understood these principles and forgiven my dad and forgiven my perceptions or "my story," we could have had a beautiful healing experience. If I had "shown up" in a different way with my dad, then maybe he would have let me see the amazing man that he was for others. NOTICE would have changed both of our lives. FORGIVENESS would have given me a gift that I can no longer have in this lifetime with him, but one that serves me every day on my own path.

Sean — **FORGIVENESS=FREEDOM**

"Are you saying we are not brothers?" Eric asked, as we both stood outside the courtroom. "You lived with them the entire time," I said. "You never suspected anything. You turned your back on dad and you haven't even been here all week for the trial. You could have seen all of the testimony for yourself. You could have seen what I've seen. The girls lied about what dad did, and they admitted they lied. I'm shocked that judge hasn't thrown it out and let Dad go home. This is a circus and the prosecutor ought to be ashamed for the things he said to mom. This is about your ex-wife trying to get money through a civil suit and embarrass mom and dad. You could have stopped this. You lived with them and if you saw anything, you would have said something. You blew this. I heard about you and your ex going to mom and dad to try to get money from them just before the charges came down. I also heard you threatened mom and dad that you would ruin their lives. No jury in their right mind could find dad guilty of this. Yes, I'm telling you we are not brothers."

The verdict was read, and my dad was found guilty on all charges against him for sexually assaulting my nieces. He was sentenced to two life sentences for doing something that the jury should have known was physically impossible. He was physically incapable of having sexual intercourse due to his paraplegia, and there was no physical evidence that any abuse had taken place. My dad was clearly guilty of taking inappropriate pictures of the girls. All I could see at the time was that he was not fit to serve jail time, and that my mother would be alone. My brother, his ex-wife, and their two daughters sat on the other side of the courtroom. There was an evil to the celebration of my father's demise amid so much reasonable doubt. I cannot describe the anger and disappointment I felt towards everyone involved. I'll never forget how my brother looked at my dad in that courtroom. I've never seen such hatred and malice in someone's eyes, which shifted to joy and lack of empathy when the verdict came down. Our father was already a paraplegic and had just been given the equivalent of a death sentence. A paraplegic would struggle to survive in prison and this truth was what seemed to give their side the most joy.

An emotionally intelligent person could not help but feel pain and sadness for both sides. The girls were victims. My father was also a victim. This event tore my entire family apart. Their side acted like there was no question that the man who had helped to raise the two girls in the absence of their father and a neglectful mother should receive nothing short of death for his transgressions. Their smiling faces seemed to show that they were able to suspend the idea that this was about real people. It was as if they had just won the lottery. All things being relative, the settlement in the civil trial years later would prove that to be true.

These are the facts: My dad was guilty of something, and the pictures were awful. His actions would lead an outsider to believe he was a pedophile. But this was my dad, and it was too hard to believe that. My focus was only on my dad and his well-being. The days following my father's incarceration were the darkest of my life and, for me at that time, forgiveness was not an option.

I spent most of the first few days trying to decide what further danger my mother was in and trying to rationalize what I perceived as an act of war against my mom and dad, from other members of my family. The girls lied about what happened. My sister-in-law was in it for the money. My brother, his ex-wife and my parents were all guilty of neglect and poor decisions that had caused all of this pain and suffering. Despite all of this, I regretted the conversation I had with my brother. I wanted nothing left unsaid with him no matter how this ended. I reached out to him through a mutual friend.

Janet,

Long story short is that I need to clear the air with my brother. I said some things to him last month at the trial that I do not mean and if we never speak again I just need to set some things straight between us. I really need to tell him I'm sorry, but I want it to come from me directly. I don't have a phone number or any way to contact my brother, and I have changed mine since we talked last. If you talk to his ex, please ask her to pass him my info. I just need a few minutes with him on the phone or email.

Thanks for any help and again sorry to drop in like this. I hope everything is going well for you and your family.

My mother was a wreck and I truthfully feared for her life as I tried to rationalize what I perceived as a systematic attack on my parents' physical, emotional, and financial well-being. It consumed me and I thought only of revenge every day. My brother, his girls, his ex, the judge, my dad's attorney, the police department, and the prosecutor had all played a part in my dad losing his freedom. I couldn't run fast enough on the treadmill or swim enough laps in the pool to make this go away.

Within six weeks, while waiting for him to get transferred from county jail to prison, we got the call that my dad was in critical condition in the ICU. "Was he attacked by another prisoner? Did the guards try to kill him? Did my brother send someone to kill my dad?" These all seemed like plausible options for my irrational mind at the time. When my mom and I got up to his room in the ICU, there was no doctor by his bedside, and he told us himself that he was dying from infections in his hips and they were going to cut off his legs to try to save him. This wasn't happening. This was further confirmation that the system was trying to kill my dad. This was my weakest moment as a man. My body grieved and could not decide whether to cry, puke, or both. I was unable to be supportive for my mom as she said goodbye to her husband. I was too weak to stand and sat down next to a trash can, watching my mom hold my dad's hand. The other prisoners in the room were dead or dying. My father was the only one who was conscious and could open his eyes. He said, "I have to go, son. I cannot survive this." I just sobbed and sobbed and told him that wasn't true, and all that matters is what you think.

I said over and over again through my sobs and slurred speech, as I tried to breath and talk, in a high-pitched sob that I couldn't recognize as my own voice, "It matters what you think! It matters what you think!" But I didn't believe myself that his thoughts could save him. I believed he wanted to die and he just waited for my mom to get there to say he loved her one last time. I wanted him to be out of pain and I WANTED TO BE OUT OF THIS PAIN. I wanted it to be over, and I just stared in disbelief as I saw life leaving my dad's body.

I felt like a coward. The fact that I could not be stronger for my mom, and say goodbye to my dad like I thought a man should, so overwhelmed me, that a piece of me died right there in that room that day. It didn't register in my mind when the guard ducked his head into the door frame of the room and informed us that our time was up. We were instructed to put our gloves, shower caps, gowns, and foot protectors in the trash can before we left the room. I was in a trance not believing that we were being told to hurry up and watch my dad die to fit in their schedule. No guard dared enter the room because of the known contagious infections. They would bark instructions from outside in the hall and we would obey. They told us we could come back tomorrow to see if my dad was still alive.

My father was being tortured to death by the prison's neglect to treat minor infections that were typical for his paralysis. He was property of the state of Texas, and we had no way to help him. The infection had gone untreated so long that it was in his blood stream and he was septic. This went on for several days and he was kept in a hospice-like environment. I was powerless as we were made to watch him waste away with subpar medical treatment. My mom had treated these types of minor infections for 25 years at home with ease. This was routine stuff, and I decided that they tried to kill him, and they were continuing to try and finish the job. This belief and lack of control caused my heart to turn black with rage.

We were able to visit him daily and each time we did, my mom and I would pray with our hands over my dad's chest. Mom prayed. I listened. I decided that God was not present with us in this situation. He would have never allowed one family to suffer so much. We'd hold my dad's hand and tell him goodbye. His hands were swollen and my mom would kiss his hands and forehead and tell him over and over that he was the best thing that ever happened to her and that she never regretted a day in her life that she spent with him. He was her heart and her life. He would whisper to my mom, and just smile at her. He was so happy knowing she was there. He'd labor to turn to his left trying to remember to look at me too. I wondered if he could see me. He'd smile at me and I'd die a little each time my heart broke over and over again as we'd watch as he breathed a deep breath expecting him to exhale for the final time.

"There is no way any human being deserves what my dad is going through right now. They will pay. This life is over. My life is over." Dad looked right at my mom and said he was sorry. He was taking his last breaths again, and my mom did something that shocked me. She leaned her head back and said in a loud accusatory voice, "And what are you sorry for? What did you do?" He whispered, "I took the pictures. I took the pictures." My mom shot back again, loudly, "And what else did you do?" My dad stared at her and said three times, "That's all. That's all. That's all." My mom said, "I know, baby. We all know." This became a daily ritual, where he lived another night and we would return and say goodbye again the next day.

To Eric's ex-wife:

This is the only way I know of to contact you. My dad is having health issues and is undergoing treatment for infections.

I have had a few visits with him and he is at peace and has forgiven my brother and the girls.

I have a concern that the girls won't be given the opportunity to recant before his death, or correct their stories. If what they have claimed is not true, and they know it, I am concerned that they may have personal issues later in life when they realize the pain they have caused. That would make these events even more devastating to both of our families. I am asking you to please talk to them again and make sure that they are clear and confident about what they testified to and what they have accused my dad of doing to them. Because they are minors, they risk nothing by clearing up any confusion or mistakes they have made. If that is the case, the time is now.

I'm hopeful that you will receive this message, and I will take a non response to this as that you have talked to them and that you and the girls are 100% confident and at peace with what is happening

to my dad. I understand the civil suit is in progress, and you may be
advised not to talk to me. Contact me in anyway if you like.
Sean

The next few months, I would fly to Houston on the weekends, visit my dad, and focus on helping my mom. It was day-to-day agony and a roller-coaster ride as my dad recovered and battled infections after both legs were amputated. It became our norm and there was some solace in the consistency of it all for me.

One night, we decided to go to a bar, and I drank beer while mom smoked cigarettes. It was odd for both of us as I never drank around her, and she hadn't smoked a cigarette in 20 years. We sat there for a few hours and I confessed to her what she already knew: There was rage in my heart, and it was growing stronger every day. With my mom, the answer to everything revolves around the church. She said she and my dad both forgave my brother, the ex and the girls the first day the allegations came down and that she never considered anything else but forgiveness because, "that's what The Word tells us, Sean, and that's what we do."

That night, back at my mom and dad's house, lying in the bed that my brother slept in as a kid, I began the practice of forgiveness. I stared at the ceiling with my eyes wide open and said, "Eric, I forgive you. Eric, I forgive you." I said it out loud over and over again. I kept repeating it until I became sleepy and lost track of when I said it last and then I'd dozed off to sleep.

The next night, it was automatic. As soon as my head hit the pillow, I started talking out loud. The words never changed, "Eric, I forgive you. Eric, I forgive you." I slept those first few nights all the way through.

For six months, I said this every night and then there were times during the day when I'd sit at my desk and cry. It always came back to the thoughts of taking revenge and I responded in the same way: "Eric, I forgive you! Eric I forgive you! I'd say it out loud and it sounded like I was shouting at the top of my lungs. Two years later, I still choose to forgive and sometimes have to talk myself to sleep in the same way. I will continue to forgive as I deal with the challenges that this situation presents. It's not going away, and neither am I. My dad remains in prison today. My mom has spent all of their savings on legal fees and settling the civil suit out of court with Eric's ex and the girls. To this day, Mom continues to give all she has and all she is to my dad. Things have settled in but as her situation worsens, it brings up old feelings that I get to deal with right away so they don't get out of hand. It also brings up new feelings towards my dad that I choose to forgive him for, too. I have had the opportunity to practice forgiveness at length with everyone who was involved in this tragedy. In the beginning, I thought my change of heart was saving other people's lives. I know now that I am the one who benefits by forgiving. Forgiveness lets me move forward and, at this time, in this situation, it is the greatest gift I could have ever given myself.

Furthermore, ONLY I could have given myself this gift.

We hear about it all the time, but if we don't do it ourselves, it doesn't get done. I may have never followed through with my destructive thoughts of getting even with all of those people, but I could have chosen not to forgive them and let this eat me up for the rest of my life. I also could have chosen to only forgive a few of those involved instead of all of them, all the time, as many times as it takes. Letting my heart be occupied with just a little bit of hatred would be the emotional equivalent of leaving your home to go on vacation after setting just a little fire in the middle of your living-room floor. There is no way to measure what we could have done in this life had we learned to forgive sooner. I spent two years being distracted by hate, fear, and sadness. That was my choice. Sometimes, I have to take the long way around even though I'm holding a map with all of the shortcuts on it. This wasn't the scenic route, and if I could go back, I would have forgiven them the first day and no doubt saved myself the bumpy ride. If I could give you one gift right now, it would be that you forgive those who have wronged you and that you honor that sometimes you can't see all of the angles until you are able to look back over time. You begin with forgiveness for those who bring you pain and sorrow today. Then you keep your eyes and your heart open so that you can know what to do next. I hope you choose a life of forgiveness. You deserve it.

SEAN OBSERVING

There have been many traumatic experiences in my life and many times that the lesson of forgiveness = freedom would have saved me grief and prevented overwhelming rage, but the story above is to date the most extreme. Forgiveness kept me sane and allows me a peace that I could never have experienced before. Let me reiterate what was said in the lesson portion. Forgiveness is not saying my brother's actions were ok. It is not saying my Dad's actions were ok. It is saying that forgiveness is the ONLY thing that will set me free and bring me peace. I choose forgiveness because it is a choice from Love and not Fear....love for me.

APPLICATION
Forgiveness = Freedom – Tool

Forgiveness is definitely a tool, a choice. When you understand the true freedom that forgiveness gives, you will wish you had applied it more frequently in your life. The freedom comes not from the accepting of the act or exonerating the person that may have caused the pain, but knowing that what matters is that you cut yourself free from the tie or cord. Allowing anger, blame, rage, and fear to run your life means you are not in control. Forgiveness is simply the tool that frees you from the chain that binds you.

The exercise below is a way to really learn empathy. Empathy is the most important of all leadership traits. The ability to walk in someone else's shoes is the fastest, most effective way to not only relate to them but to forgive them. The truth is someone is always going through something. At times, our circumstances overwhelm us. It doesn't matter how insignificant we think the other's experience is. This is not a game of comparison and each individual's situation holds merit and is equally important. The cheerleader who is cut from the squad before her senior year experiences a loss and devastation that is on the same level as the person who loses a family member in a car accident. When we learn how to empathize and we PRACTICE it, life changes instantly.

EXERCISE: Forgiveness = Freedom

SUPPLIES: Pen and paper, or a computer

APPROX. TIME: 45 minutes

PURPOSE: Once an event has been neutralized, forgiveness is a tool that allows you to cut the cord that has tied you to the event. Forgiveness is the final step in clearing the slate for creating intentionally the life you desire. The exercise below is one tool that might support you with forgiveness.

ACTION: Complete both Part 1 and Part 2.

Part 1 –

On the bottom left hand side of a large piece of paper write your birthday. Draw a line from that date up and down like a curvy road till it ends on the bottom right hand side of the paper where you will write today's date. At the halfway point on the road you will mark the year that is half of your age. You are creating a memory map. Your assignment is to mark different points in your life that were challenging or caused pain *(examples: parents got divorced, didn't make the cheerleading squad, first big heartbreak, got fired, etc.)*

For each mark, Be the Observer, and decide if there is anyone or anything to forgive. If the answer is yes, then circle that event. Many times the painful events in our lives will involve our parents. We ask that you consider completing the next part of this exercise for one if not both of your parents. It can also be used for anyone, even casual acquaintances that have caused you upset.

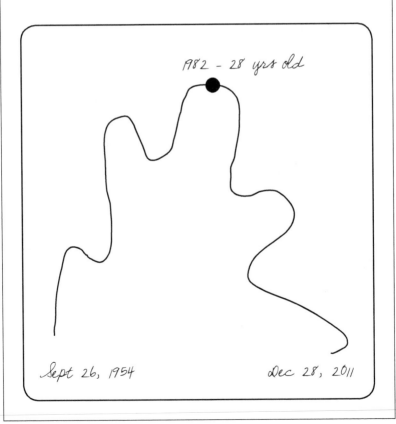

1982 - 28 yrs old

Sept 26, 1954

Dec 28, 2011

Part 2 –

This next section is called, **"Walking in Someone Else's Shoes."**

At the top of a page, write "Walking in _____'s Shoes." Write the person's name in the blank.

You will be writing this document in the first person of the one you are needing to forgive or possibly understand better. You will begin with the basic facts. This example below is Sean's mother.

As you begin to write their story, which for many of our parents, might include poverty or challenging times, you may begin to feel empathy for some of their actions and attitudes.

"Walking in Francyne Terry Eubanks' Shoes"

I was born to two loving parents on Sept 26, 1954. My Dad was in the navy and my Mom stayed home to take care of me. I was a happy little girl until at 10 years old, my Mother died. This hurt my Dad so much that I guess he couldn't stand that I reminded him of my Mom, so he left. I was alone and literally living on the street at age 10. How quickly life can change! I'd go from foster home to foster home and then stay with family and friends in Austin. I was alone, frightened, and had no sense of home until some dear friends took me in to live with them. My Dad drank a lot, was never around and, at the age of 13, I realized that he didn't want me.

I was tall and good at basketball and could make friends easily, so I guessed I'd be ok. I struggled to stay focused and dropped out of school in 10th grade. I felt like a burden on those around me and wanted my independence so I went to work as a waitress. I moved in with a guy and the next thing you know, I'm pregnant and I'm only 16 years old. He wants nothing to do with the baby, so I decide to raise it on my own. I'm overwhelmed with being a mother at such a young age and having a bi-racial child is none too easy.

I fall in love with this guy, Donnie. He has hair down to his waist and he fights a lot. He's a wild man, but I like that. We decided to get married and he said he would raise my daughter as his own. We soon found out that we couldn't support a child and I made the decision to give my daughter up for adoption.

My new husband and I would continue to struggle to make ends meet, but my daughter went to a stable home with a family that could take care of her. I thought with previous health issues I would be unable to bear more children. We were wrong, and I was pregnant with my oldest son, Eric, in 1974. Nineteen months after he was born, we had our second son, Sean. We had two beautiful boys and the year was 1976. Though life was hard and we were broke, we were a family.

Five years later, Sean had a head injury that shook us up, and by the end of that same year, my husband Donnie was paralyzed from the waist down in a car accident. He could no longer earn a living in construction so we lived off of Social Security in a trailer. Life got more and more difficult until a settlement came years later from the insurance company of the man who was at fault for the car accident. We had enough money to move and start a new life. We had the means to send our boys to good schools and we moved into a golf-course community that was a far cry from the trailer park.

My husband was an entrepreneur and a giver. He invested in real estate and built our wealth with ease. Over the next 20 years, my husband would have 17 major surgeries and I would spend most of my time being his nurse. He was unable to function properly from the waist down and he needed lots of help with basics. We kept this private and did not burden our kids with this information.

My sons were wild in high school and were likeable but often focused on being the life of the party. They took after their dad and I assumed they would outgrow it one day. I became a grandmother at 35 years old, but my son was not ready to be a father. My youngest son, Sean, went off to college, while Eric continued to live with us off and on. He was a late bloomer, and I thought for a long time his shortcomings were my fault. He got caught drug trafficking in Mexico and, after a year and half, we were finally able to buy his way out of prison.

Not long after that, I was a grandmother again but this time to two twin girls. My other son, Sean, had left for college after his senior year of high school and rarely came home to visit. Eric and his wife divorced soon after the girls were born but we'd carry on and help with the girls in every way possible. It seemed that Eric still wasn't ready or able to be a father. So my husband and I would step in and fill the void. Life was good, and the girls were difficult, but we had been young parents, too, and would help our son and ex daughter-in-law every way we could.

I was approached by the mother of the 2 girls and asked if we would set up a trust fund for the children to make up for the missed child support. We always did everything we could to help her, and yet she was resentful and angry. Soon thereafter she filed charges of child *abuse against my husband. The police came to our home to arrest him in front of all of our neighbors. I was embarrassed, but wasn't worried because I knew of my husband's inability to do what he was accused of. I felt like it was impossible to gain a conviction, and soon the mother of the girls would be exposed for the extortion attempt. But that was not the case. My husband was convicted, and we lost everything. The civil suit was filed at the same time as the criminal case. My husband is appealing the convictions, and I will continue to support him. I have faith in Jesus above all else and know this is all happening for a reason. I'm starting a new business and adjusting to my new life. I am surrounded by great friends and I am up for the challenges ahead. I'm 56 and get to reinvent myself. I'm a strong woman with unshakable faith.*

Another example – Leslie's neighbor:
When you use this exercise for someone in a current situation, you may choose to gear the description of their life to what is applicable to the event and what might be driving their actions. This example is Leslie's neighbor.

SYNOPSIS – My neighbor, Carla, is always showing up unexpectedly and uninvited to my home. I think she watches out her window for me to pull in the driveway. Whether I am kind or abrupt, she will find a way to push herself into my home almost every evening.

"Walking in Carla's Shoes"

My name is Carla and I am a 58-year-old woman. I have lived in this house since I bought it at the age of 35. I have never been married nor had children. I have worked for Tyson Electric as a bookkeeper for the past 30 years. My best friend is my cat. Her name is Samantha. My life is orderly and everything is in its' place. My days and nights have been the same for the past 23 years, ever since my parents died and I moved into this house.

Ok, I admit it: I am lonely. Samantha is great and my TV shows are great, but I am beginning to wonder if there is not more to life than security and routine. My next door neighbor's life is anything but secure and routine. There are people coming and going all the time. Her roommate has those three teenage boys, and they have all kinds of friends. She must spend a ton of money at the grocery store, because she is always feeding people day and night. I don't know how she stands it, and, for whatever reason, I cannot stay away.

I know I am being a nuisance. I can tell by how she is always trying to sneak in when I cross her yard, but I just want to be a part of all that chaos. When I am in their kitchen I am just not as lonely..

TONE: Thoughtful and sincere

DEBRIEF: Being aware of another's experience allows you the opportunity to look at an event from 360 degrees. It allows you the opportunity to feel empathy and possibly make it easier to let go and forgive. Also it is not necessary to know the details of their life. It is enough to imagine what they might be feeling to open the door of empathy that will change any relationship and bring you peace.

TAKEAWAY: When you can stop in a moment and put yourself in another's shoes, you have the gift of using empathy to free yourself from pain through forgiveness. Empathy is the key cornerstone of genuine, human relationships.

" Remembering that I'll be dead soon is the most important thing I've ever encountered to help me make the big choices in life, because almost everything–all external expectations, all pride, all fear of embarrassment or failure–these things just fall away in the face of death, leaving only what is truly important. You are already naked. There is no reason not to follow your heart. „

– STEVE JOBS

Living "As If"

Your Thoughts Create Your Life...all the time. To know what you are thinking you learn to **Be the Observer** – to step back and view, with **No Judgment**, your thoughts and actions. Now that you can view an event or a thought, you have the ability to **Neutralize** it and then **Choose** what it will be or mean to you; to lighten the load choose **Freedom through Forgiveness** and when the slate is clean you create through **Intention**.

The Webster definition of intention is—*a determination to act a certain way; to be deliberate and on purpose*. Intention is about experiencing your goal "as if" it has already happened. Stephen Covey refers to it as "begin with the end in mind." Getting clear concerning what you desire, living in a place as if your dreams had already arrived; that is Intention.

Lessons 1 through 6 are necessary work to clear the slate for creating. The hard work is done. Now the fun begins.

There have been a number of movies produced and books written in the last few years on the law of attraction. Most of us think in terms of the material things we desire. I want a red car, I envision it, I put pictures on the wall and, bam, it shows up. Sometimes this works. But life is so much more complicated than getting the new red car you desire.

Life is mostly made up of relationships and experiences, the subtle nuances of getting along with your boss. What to do when your teenager comes home late with alcohol on his breath. How to react when your wife tells you she has breast cancer. What to do when you've lost your job and they foreclose on your home. This is what really makes up our lives and, for every one of these examples, there is a clean and clear path to take using Intention.

Leslie - I can't remember a time in my life, before I reached the age of 40 where anyone asked me to define who I was and what I wanted out of life. I was a Christian and tried to live my life as much as possible through the example of Jesus, but I was still pretty vague on the woman I wanted to be. What did Leslie, who is a middle-aged, divorced, single mom believe about herself and the world? What did she stand for? How did she want her life to look? What would they say for her eulogy? Sean took on this exercise for himself after the death of my husband in 2007 and shares his eulogy in the story below.

When we work with teens and adults, we will have them create a contract or a creed for how they will live their life. We make decisions every day based on "What will people think?"

Or "What is the least amount of work I can do to get by?" Or "What can I get away with without anyone knowing?" We may never have made a conscious decision to write down what we stand for and what we want to represent to the world.

In the movie, "Coach Carter," Denzel Washington plays a basketball coach hired to shake up the team in a school that is in a pretty rough part of town. He has strict rules and asks the students to sign a contract where they agree to be on time for all practices, to wear a coat and tie on game days, and to keep a 2.5 grade point average. When their grades fall below this, he locks the gym door and lets them know they won't play again until their grades improve. The teachers agree to stay after school and tutor the kids. He lands the lesson that they signed a contract and their word is their word no matter how tough the consequences.

You can imagine the uproar from the students and the parents in the movie. This is such a powerful lesson for all of us. Your word is your word. A contract is a legal, binding agreement and Coach Carter was not going to break it, or let the players break it, despite the fact that the team was headed to the State finals and would lose their position if they missed its games.

How many of us ever consciously decide that we are going to be a certain type of person and that we will keep that contract with ourselves, as if it were legal and binding in a court of law? We ask our workshop participants to create a Core Value Contract, an agreement that they have with themselves. After cleaning the slate and understanding that they are creating their lives, they get the chance to decide exactly what kind of life they are going to create.

These contracts are powerful and set the bar for every decision they will make. An example might be…I STAND FOR LOVE, JUSTICE, AND FORGIVENESS or I STAND FOR PEACE, LOYALTY, AND FREEDOM.

Once you know the type of person you want to be in the world and you create a contract with yourself, you can then choose your reactions, your perceptions and your decisions to be in alignment with your contract. This simple tool can have the choice you need to make stick out loud and clear. You make one very important decision – Who am I going to be? And then every other choice you make in life must be in alignment with your contract. This is a very important piece of creating an intentional life. Another important concept is "Living as If."

"Living As If" can be easily explained like this: If you want to be a district manager of your company, you would use this concept by applying the definition (act a certain way). You must act like a district manager, display their characteristics and traits, and simply BE that position. "Living As If" works for everything: being a district manager, the best parent, a loving husband or wife, a healthy contributor to society—everything. You bring your desires into your life by BEING them or "Living as If."

Intention is the final piece, but the most important of all. This is it! We now know that we can create any life we desire to have, regardless of circumstances. It is 100% up to us, every day, 24/7. We find this concept unbelievably freeing. We can be any kind of person we desire and have amazing relationships. We can wake up every day loving our lives. If these lessons can create such peace and joy for us, what might they do for you?

Leslie — LIVING "AS IF"

"Leslie, I am Sherry, a friend of your son, David. I hate to have to tell you this, but David is in the hospital. He has been committed to the mental ward at the UNC Hospital in Chapel Hill." "What are you talking about? What happened?" I said. "We found him hiding behind our house. He was naked and had cuts all over his body from running through the woods. He had been up for days and had apparently been doing a mixture of drugs with one of his friends. I couldn't get him to come in the house and we ended up calling the police. I'm so sorry, Ms. Palmer. I didn't know what else to do. We thought he was going to hurt himself," Sherry sobbed into the phone. "You did the right thing. I'll get there as soon as I can," I said.

Joe and I were volunteering with his daughter, Jennifer, in Austin. I screamed for him to get down off the building of the nonprofit he was roofing and explained the situation. Jennifer went into action. She got me on a plane to Atlanta that was leaving within the hour. There were no flights that night from Atlanta to Raleigh, but the next morning, I caught the first flight out.

My baby. My baby. That is all I could say. My chest was tight, and my stomach would not stay in one place. I could hardly breathe. It's not that this was a complete surprise. I knew that somehow the horror of the last year would come to a head in some fashion, but I didn't expect it to be this extreme.

Let me go back a few years and explain. David is my only son and, I know I am his mother, but I think most would agree that he is an exceptionally wonderful young man. David is extremely intelligent and graduated from UNC-Chapel Hill with Highest Honors, or Summa Cum Laude. He is a gifted writer, artist, tall, good-looking, and funny with a gentle loving disposition. The years at UNC were full of service as he was a sponsor for many in AA. David got sober at 19. After a DUI and some tough conversations, David went into a recovery program following his freshman year of college. It was during this time that I learned much about my son that broke my heart for him and myself. I was very involved in the family sessions and other programs that he took for his own growth. It was during that year that David and I truly got to know each other's hearts and this experience was key for me in deciding to create the Quest Teen Leadership workshops. David staffed many of our trainings through the years, and this work and living the lessons taught in this handbook are a huge part of both of our lives.

In David's senior year of college he decided that he had taken on the label of alcoholic too soon. After informing me, his sponsors, and friends in AA, he decided to have a beer. Needless to say, it did not end with just one. He quickly began to spiral to heavy drinking, but was able to maintain himself enough to graduate college. By the end of the summer he was all but homeless and had gotten his second DUI citation. I remember going to visit him in Chapel Hill. (I was living in Atlanta at the time.) I was calling all the important people in his life to prepare for an intervention. He knew something was up and he told me that if I continued, he would walk away and I would never see him again.

The months that followed were brutal for me. Something was not quite right with him and I knew it was more than the drinking. He went to work in New Orleans to help with the Katrina cleanup, and I visited him over Thanksgiving. He seemed lost and shaky but was not ready to seek help.

When I got to the hospital that next morning, no one would admit that he was a patient. Apparently there are rules concerning privacy of patients in the mental wards. "I have been up for 24 hours and I need to see my son!!!" They didn't care. Without the code they would not even confirm he was in that hospital. Thank God Sherry walked up just as I was losing it a bit with the receptionist. Since Sherry was the one who had him committed, she was allowed to get me an access code.

As we walked into David's room, I could not believe my eyes. He looked beautiful. He was clean shaven and his eyes were clear. He hugged me and whispered in my ear. "Has the world ended yet?" "There are helicopters following me. Look out the window and tell me what's going on out there."

I was very calm and assured him that all was well. He spoke in a very calm manner about the people that had been following him and that he wasn't sure we were safe in the hospital. I'm not exactly sure how I knew to simply agree and maintain a calm demeanor, but I knew that my David was just not "there" and that keeping him calm was the best thing.

"Ms. Palmer, David has had a complete break from reality. We are not sure what has caused this to happen. It could be a combination of drugs that he has taken or he might be bipolar or schizophrenic. He may never regain his sanity and might stay like this forever," said the incredibly young, insensitive psychiatrist that set across from me.

"Are you freaking kidding me? He's been here all of 24 hours and you make this assessment?" I yelled. "Well, I just want you prepared for what might happen," he replied. "How long does he have to stay here, what is the procedure, what comes next?" I replied in a calmer manner.

"He needs to stay the rest of the week and we will keep him medicated and talk about outpatient treatment possibilities."

At that moment, all I knew was that there was no way my son was going to be scared and lost the rest of his life. That was not an option. I would research until I found a solution to get my son back to the David that I knew so well. Whatever IT was that had him, IT was not going to keep him.

This was the beginning of a very long road. The lessons taught in this book are the only thing that kept me sane. Dozens of times a day, I would picture my son, healthy, married, and holding his child. This is the vision I would hold for him. This was my intention. I would live "as if."

Joe and I spent the next year taking care of David. It was March of 2006, and we were still on our honeymoon. After marrying on February 14, 2006, we sold our homes and bought an RV. It was our intention to travel around the country providing Quest teen workshops, and we had just completed one in Lake Village, AK, earlier that month. When I told Joe about David's condition, his first words were, "We will provide a home for him with us in Dallas." My husband had sold his business and all his possessions to create this new life for us on the road. This was his dream. We were so excited about living in the RV and traveling and teaching, but without hesitation he was willing to give all that up to take care of my child whom he had only met once. This man was truly an angel.

The next year was extremely hard. There were times when David walked out of the house and I did not know if I would ever see him again. It took months and much care for David to heal. We bought a condo and Joe went back to work and David went with him every day. How can I best describe Joe? He owned a roofing company and drove a Ford F350. He wore the equivalent of a cowboy hat and was Texas through and through. But there was this gentle poetic side to him. He was an amazing writer and shared inspiration from his heart through emails to those he loved. He could meditate for hours and sought peace and calm in every situation.

At the funeral David spoke about his experience with Joe. "Tap, tap, tap. That is what I hear every morning at 6 a.m." "Time to create an amazing day," whispered Joe through the door of David's room. "What exciting things will we experience today?" or "Let's go in this Quiktrip and get a Slurpee and send love to everyone we see," David shared at the funeral. Everyone laughed as they pictured this tough-looking Texas man spreading love through his thoughts. "There is not a motivational book on tape that I have not heard. And although at 6:30 in the morning,

I was not always excited about listening to Eckhart Tolle, this daily ritual with Joe healed my mind and my heart. Joe Crow, saved my life," shared David, as tears streamed down his face.

When I think about the year and eight months I had with my husband and that a year and seven months were basically dedicated to helping my son heal his life, I know that Joe was a gift, an angel. When people are aghast at the tragedy of our love story I let them know I CHOOSE only to see the gift. Joe was a gift. His death, David's sickness were neutral events. Joe gave me back my son, and anyone who knows me knows he could have not given me a greater gift.

I set my intention for the woman I am going to be: a woman who is comfortable in her skin, a woman who doesn't waste time worrying about what others might think. Someone who chooses to be joyous, loving and connected to all as I know that people are more alike than we are different. I am a woman who takes all the events in my life and sees the good, the gift. I am a mother, daughter, partner, and friend who chooses to teach these lessons to others.

Although I am not this woman in every moment, I catch myself pretty quickly and know from experience that if I choose to come from this place, I am happier and life just seems to flow more easily. The decisions I have to make, whether big or small, are pretty easy. When you take a choice and line it up next to your intention, there is often a pretty clear path. And when there isn't, I listen to my heart and choose from Love, knowing that everything works out exactly as it's supposed to.

LESLIE OBSERVING

When the events in your life are completely out of your control, it is easy to let yourself spiral into an emotional hell. Dealing with mental illness in a loved one and the complete helplessness you feel is an almost unbearable situation. The ability to Be the Observer, to step back and view my thoughts with no judgment, and make decisions that are in alignment with my contract once again saved my life and kept me sane.

Not only did the tool BEING THE OBSERVER help me focus on the thoughts that would keep me aligned with my contract, it also allowed me to remember that my thoughts create my life and that I need not accept the words of another as truth. I could make up my own story or interpretation of the event.

Whereas many might use intention to create a new job or a new car, it can be used daily in shifting your energy from all the things you DON'T want in your life to all the things you DO. My son is now healthy and happy and preparing for graduate school. Did my intention make that magically happen? Maybe or maybe not, but all I know is it kept me peaceful and sane and that attitude helped me deal with the circumstances in a way that supported healing.

Sean — LIVING "AS IF"

I feel like I've squeezed five lifetimes into this one already. I live my life with a sense of urgency and I act as if I have a short time left here on earth. I take risks and if my heart compels me to do something, I do it. I've always been amazed that I meet the most incredible people and come across the best opportunities when I'm attempting to contribute to something greater than myself. When I started dedicating my spare time to working on my own nonprofit and was outwardly focused on helping people, that is when my life started to change. I would find myself sitting at a charity dinner with some incredible people and wonder "How did I get here?"

I was introduced to Leslie, who had years of experience in the nonprofit world, as someone who might be able to advise me as I learned the ins and outs of running my own organization. I was so impressed with the idea of what she was teaching that I had to check it out. Volunteering to "teach" in the teen workshops with Leslie allowed me to learn some of the most important lessons of my life. I knew that her message was saving these kids' lives. I walked out of my first workshop with the knowledge I needed to live the life I had always known was possible. After seeing hundreds of kids go through the transformation, I was convinced that everyone should have access to this information and that if teenagers could be empowered, and get inspiration, confidence, and clarity from this training at the most challenging times of their lives, then adults could take this in and self-actualize as well. I was one of those adults.

The more I taught, the more I learned. I wanted to help in every way I could and I wanted to find funding to have every kid in my nonprofit be able to have a chance to attend a training. I enjoyed presenting and teaching and was a natural. With the death of Leslie's husband, Joe Crow, everything changed. I attended the funeral that was standing-room only. The line of people there to say goodbye to Joe and to support Leslie was literally a mile long. I went there to support Leslie, as I had never met Joe. She spoke about her husband in a way I'd never heard anyone speak before. It was the most authentic expression of love and grief I had ever seen. "Was it possible that a woman could love a man that much?" "Did he know...surely he knew... there is nothing left unsaid between the ones we love...that's in the training...of course he knew". I heard Joe's son, Thomas, acknowledge what the trainings had done to strengthen their relationship and how great the last few years had been between them. He talked about the bridges Joe built and the walls he let down for their relationship to grow. He loved and respected his father. "Could I say that about my dad? Would my dad say that about me? If I ever had a son, would I be the kind of dad Joe was? Could anyone say these things about me if I died tomorrow? Have I done enough to make an impact on anyone's life?"

I knew the answers to these questions, but I did not want to face them. I did some soul searching and decided to face my shortcomings and write an honest assessment of my life. Nothing gave me more clarity about how I wanted to live going forward than writing my own eulogy:

SEAN EUBANKS – *"September 29, 1976-January 23, 2008"*

Sean Eubanks was a go-getter. He was constantly on the move, trying to make things happen. His smile lit up a room. He wore his emotions on his sleeve. When he was having a great day, he shared it with everyone. When he was having a bad day, he didn't need to say a word; everybody around him knew to stay away. He was an athlete through and through. He pushed himself physically and never considered any limitations. He ran a marathon, was a national karate champion, and played college football. He was a risk taker in business and in his personal life. When he traveled, he made sure every day was an adventure. He dove face-to-face with great white sharks, surfed along the entire east coast of Australia, and crossed South Africa in a pair of flip-flops and a backpack.

He once said that he was much more fearful of this life than of the prospect of his death. After spending months abroad, he would return with the realization that he was wasting his life in America chasing a buck. Although Sean loved this country and was proud to be a Texan, he was not so keen on our western shortcomings and was suspicious of Christianity. He prided himself on never eating fast food, and thought very little of "fat, ignorant America." He lived in Thailand for a while and through his travels in Asia, grew to appreciate the Asian culture.

He fell in love three times early in his life and spent the rest of his life avoiding long-term relationships at all costs. He didn't trust women. He used his travels to escape from the everyday grind and was honest about the fact he was searching for something. He once said that he literally circled this globe and couldn't find what he was looking for. His cousin, Dee, once called him a lost soul, which he admitted was true.

He jumped into every task and venture with all of his heart and all of his being. He wanted to be known as a giver, so he founded Kick 4 College. He refused to accept mediocrity and knew that whatever he did was worth doing well, or not doing at all. He judged himself by what he knew he was capable of and rarely stopped for a second to let acknowledgement in. He stayed busy with work. The next task or the next project was what he used to hide from relationships. He was sociable, witty, funny, and smart, but rarely opened his heart to those around him. He was a tough guy that prided himself on being independent. He was a fighter who struggled to trust his fellow man.

Sean loved his mother and father more than anything. He wanted to make them proud. He was aware of their many struggles and vowed to never struggle as they did. He aimed to advance the Eubanks name, to put it in a place for all to see that The Eubanks had arrived. His biggest fear was going broke. He came to realize near the end that to really live this life is to love another human being and be loved in return. In the last few months of his life, he made great strides in creating intimacy with his family and I am grateful to have known him as he truly was: authentic, open, trusting, and loving.

I didn't enjoy what I had written about myself. It's true I had done a lot of exciting things in my life, but hadn't really made much of a difference. I came away from this experience determined to change and rewrite my eulogy. I reconnected with my family, started a new business, and had an incredible event that year with my nonprofit. Later in the year, my family and I took a vacation to Irvine, CA, where I was inducted into the Martial Arts Hall of Fame. Life was just getting better and better. I had no idea that it would be our last vacation as a family.

Within months, my dad was in prison, my family at war with each other and my business was bankrupt. I now know that life will have its ups and downs, but going forward, I know I will always have control of my thoughts and the ability to see beyond my circumstances to intentionally create the life I want to live. I look forward to what's next in every aspect of my life. We are picking up the pieces of what is left of my family. My business is doing well. My nonprofit will have another big event soon and I'm writing this book with my dear friend, Leslie.

I have the privilege of setting my intention for what the rest of my life will be. I have Leslie to thank for exposing me to this powerful message through the Quest trainings. I can't tell you what will happen next with my family, what business opportunity is right around the corner, or what's going to happen to our economy, but I can tell you that I choose to create a life of love, commitment, and freedom without regret.

SEAN OBSERVING

What could be more powerful than being able to create your own eulogy? I mean creating it before you die, so you still have time to make sure you were the man or woman you wanted to be. Each of us has that opportunity every day. We create the person we are by our thoughts, actions, and words. But so few of us intentionally decide what we are going to be. I always knew how to intentionally be the best at a sport or in business, but to intentionally create who I would BE in the world, that is relatively new.

I now make most of my decisions based on the question, "Does this choice line up with my contract?" I want a big life. Mediocrity is not in my vocabulary, and as I stated at the beginning of this book, these are innate traits. Deciding to BE a man that is Open, Loving, and Trusting (my contract) is a choice and my intention.

APPLICATION
Living "As If" – Home

This is not a LAW or a TOOL, this is HOME. Much like home on any website or digital device, this is the place you always go when you need to decide what to do next or where to go when you are lost. Intention is WHO you are and WHAT you want to Be, Do, and Have. This is your baseline for all decisions.

We sincerely ask that you take the time to do this application. Whereas all of the other lessons are critical in living life smoothly and clearing anything that might get in the way, this lesson must be given the proper attention. Getting clarity in your intention will have you focus your thoughts and create quicker and more deliberately. Besides, it's really fun to think big and put on paper everything you want your life to be.

EXERCISE: Living "As If"

SUPPLIES: Pen and paper, or a computer

APPROX. TIME: 20 minutes

PURPOSE: To create a template for your life using a poetically beautiful, ancient method, the eulogy. "Seeing from the end" will aid you in making choices along the path of your life. When you don't know what to do or which way to go, you can return to HOME or your intention for the answers.

ACTION: Using the template and example below, create a eulogy for yourself. Write it as if you were reading it at the funeral of your dearest friend or loved one. Put aside anything like humility or limiting beliefs. This eulogy is about you, but you are writing from the perspective of your dearest friend. Presume that you have lived a long, healthy life, and cover all important areas: family, friends, personal accomplishments, career, travel and purpose. Be true to yourself and document the life you truly desire to have and the attributes by which you want to be remembered.

....

LESLIE PALMER – *"December 18, 1959 - March 13, 2049"*

I am honored to give the eulogy of my best friend, Leslie. We were friends for over 50 years, and I know her as well as I know myself. She was always one to follow her heart. She had no fear when it came to following her dreams. She did not care what others thought of her ac-

tions and choices. Back in the early 2000s when she sold her home and quit her job to start the Quest Teen workshops, many of us thought she had lost her mind. "You're 40, girlfriend. It's time to worry about retirement and your 401k. You can't risk all your savings to start a program for teens. It's too risky." But she did, and here we are celebrating the life she created.

Leslie knew love. She gave her heart freely and experienced much love—romantic, family, friendship, and partnership.

Leslie lived what she taught. She had total clarity that her thoughts create her life and was at all times responsible for the life she was living. She was mostly filled with joy but on occasion experienced sadness. Still she was always a cup-half-full girl and would rather be happy and laughing than anyone I knew.

Leslie experienced adventure. Her bags were always packed, and she traveled the world teaching, speaking, and just having fun.

Leslie was a best-selling author. Despite being told that she couldn't write when she was 15, she went on to publish many books. Thank goodness SHE decided that she could write.

Leslie was a mother to many. She adored her son, David, and credits him for her courage to follow the path she did for the last 50 years. She loved her stepchildren and was a mother figure to hundreds who she taught over the years.

Leslie was spiritual. Anyone who knew her knew her love of God—not a religious God, but the God that lives in all of us and that loves unconditionally.

If you were her friend, you can count yourself lucky, as she was loyal, authentic, and always there for you when you needed support.

The gift she left the world was how to create an amazing life, regardless of circumstance. She lived her contract and Stood For Love, Justice and Contribution. Her body is gone and maybe her spirit, but her laughter and life's work will be with us forever.

....

TONE: Deliberate, creative, light and serious where applicable

DEBRIEF: Feel free to change your eulogy to include things that might come to mind at a later date or if your life circumstances change. This can be a working document and a constant map to keep you on track in your DAILY life for creating your BIG amazing life. Your eulogy is a verbal vision board and contract written from your heart, the best place to create.

TAKEAWAY: Seeing from the end allows you to "live as if," to walk around BEING the life you want to create in the future.

" Don't ask yourself what the
world needs. Ask yourself what
makes you come alive and
go do that, because what the
world needs is people who
have come alive. „

— JOHN ELDREDGE

Now What?

Before we give you a brief idea of how you might want to begin using these lessons, we want to thank you from the bottom of our hearts for allowing us to share our vision and our stories with you. We know some of you may have shared some of our life experiences, felt empathy for our neutral events and hopefully derived inspiration from our lessons learned. We feel such gratitude for the gift of our journeys and the opportunity to share them with you.

In our workshops, we share with students the gifts we see in them. This is done early on the first day and then, on a more personal basis, at the end of the second day. When we share, after only three hours into the training, these gifts, they are surprised and often say, "But, you don't know me." But do we really have to know them to know that they are capable of amazing feats? Capable of creating any life they choose?

For those of you who have chosen to read our book, we would like to share The Gifts We See in You:

"*You are a seeker and as such you will always find the right book, quote, movie, workshop or teacher, always at the perfect time. You have all the gifts you need to create an amazing life. You are patient and able to laugh at yourself and forgive, forgive, forgive. You are gaining clarity for the man or woman you want to be and for the life you are going to create. You stand tall in knowing you are responsible at all times for your thoughts. You are not a victim. You are living a life where everything is a choice and you choose love.*"

These are the gifts we see in you. Not really any magic here folks. Anyone reading this book is capable of being all we wrote above.

Ok, now what?

If you have not completed the exercises from the applications above, please consider doing them at least once. In the workshops, the lessons are taught in the order in the book. One suggestion would be to do one of the applications everyday for a week then use them as needed.

WE WANT TO HEAR YOUR STORIES!

We would also like that you "share" stories from your life where you used the tools from the lessons. You can share these on our website at **thinkorswim.tv**!

 Also "like" our facebook page ***Think or Swim* Book**!

Share your stories, learn about programs offered and read our blog at:

www.thinkorswim.tv

WORKSHOPS

We offer Think or Swim workshops and speaking engagements for businesses, organizations, and schools. Visit our website for more information or contact us at **info@thinkorswim.tv**
Quest Teen Leadership workshops mentioned in the book are now being offered under the Think or Swim brand.

FUTURE SERIES

Upcoming books and workshops for entrepreneurs, single parents, teens, teachers, and married couples that will include "real-life" stories from each arena are in process.

PRODUCTS

Apps for phones will help people use these tools while on the go. Additionally, games for the cell phone or laptop will make these concepts more accessible to young people, while board games will create learning opportunities for families. Furthermore, the exercises at the end of the book can be completed and shared through social media networks.

ADVENTURE TRIPS

There is no better way to learn and integrate the lessons in this book than experientially. The world travelers from our Think or Swim team will lead adventures in beautiful destinations and exotic countries. Imagine traveling with like-minded people, exploring new lands, experiencing growth and fun, and making amazing new friends.

REALITY TELEVISION

We are creating an applicable treatment for the participants in a reality television series. Using the lessons taught daily in a home or work environment will give viewers the opportunity to "see" how it all really plays out on a daily basis.

Share your stories, learn about programs offered
and read our blog at:

www.thinkorswim.tv

THINK or SWIM...*the CHOICE is yours!*

Leslie Palmer

· Creator of motivational workshops for teens, teachers, parents, and other adults
· Speaker and group discussion facilitator
· Business and relationship coach
· Mother of 30-year-old son, now a medical student
· World traveler
· Author of forthcoming book for children that teaches the life-enhancing principle—*"your thoughts create your life"*—in a fun and entertaining way

Leslie is an accomplished business executive, entrepreneur, and visionary who has launched and managed several businesses and nonprofit organizations over her 25-plus year career. In 2004, she created the nonprofit organization, Quest Teen Leadership, to empower and challenge young people to make a positive difference in the world by consciously choosing self-respect, integrity, empathy, and accountability. Since its inception, Quest has trained more than 4,000 teens across the country. The two-day workshops are now being offered through the Think or Swim brand. Leslie also has extensive experience coaching victims of physical and sexual abuse, alcoholism, drug addiction, and mental health problems, such as eating disorders, depression, and bipolar disorder.

Sean Eubanks

· Entrepreneur
· Martial Arts Hall of Famer
· Has backpacked in 40 countries
· Scuba diving instructor in Thailand
· Quest Teen Leadership training facilitator
· Introduced Congressman Ron Paul at the GOP debate in Greenville, SC, in 2011
· Author of forthcoming book for entrepreneurs

Sean has a wide-ranging background that includes business startups, real-estate lending and investing, consumer lending, public speaking, philanthropy and leadership training. In 2008, Sean launched a construction company with no capital or industry experience and turned it into $4 million-plus enterprise. His award-winning residential fence and patio company, is the fastest-growing and most profitable of its kind in the Dallas-Fort Worth area. Sean started Kick 4 College, a nonprofit martial arts scholarship league in 2007, and has grown the tournaments from 25 participants playing in high-school gymnasiums to 650 participants competing at The American Airlines Center in Dallas. He was inducted into the Martial Arts Hall of Fame in 2008 for founding the first martial arts league that awards college scholarships.

CPSIA information can be obtained
at www.ICGtesting.com
Printed in the USA
BVHW04s1735110918
527178BV00010B/55/P